Roy Acuff's Nashville

Roy Acuff's Nashville

The Life and Good Times of Country Music

Roy Acuff with William Neely

A PERIGEE BOOK

Perigee Books
are published by
The Putnam Publishing Group
200 Madison Avenue
New York, New York 10016

The author gratefully acknowledges permission from the following
sources to reprint material in their control:

Acuff-Rose Publications, Inc., 2510 Franklin Road, Nashville, Tennessee 37204, for "How's the World Treating You" by Boudleaux Bryant and
Chet Atkins. Copyright © 1952, 1953 and 1959, renewed 1980 and 1981
by Acuff-Rose Publications, Inc.; and for "Tennessee Waltz" by Redd
Stewart and Pee Wee King. Copyright © 1948, renewed 1975 by Acuff-
Rose Publications, Inc. All rights reserved. Used by permission of the
publisher.

Fred Rose Music, Inc., 2510 Franklin Road, Nashville, Tennessee
37204, for "I'm So Lonesome I Could Cry" by Hank Williams. Copyright ©
1949 by Fred Rose Music, Inc., renewed 1976, assigned to Fred Rose
Music, Inc. and Hiriam Music, Inc. for the U.S.A. only; and for "You Win
Again" by Hank Williams, copyright © 1952 by Fred Rose Music, Inc.,
copyright renewed 1980, assigned to Fred Rose Music, Inc. and Hiriam
Music, Inc. for the U.S.A. only. All rights outside the U.S.A. controlled
by Fred Rose Music, Inc. All rights reserved. Used by permission of
the publisher.

Designed by Richard Oriolo

Library of Congress Cataloging in Publication Data

Acuff, Roy.
Roy Acuff's Nashville.

1. Acuff, Roy. 2. Country musicians—United States—
Biography. 3. Country music—United States—History and
criticism. 4. Grand ole opry (Radio program) I. Neely,
William. II. Title.
ML410.A168A3   1983   784.5'2'00924 [B]   83-8109
ISBN 0-399-50874-0

First Perigee printing, 1983.

Printed in the United States of America.

1 2 3 4 5 6 7 8 9

What a beautiful thought I am thinking
  Concerning the Great Speckled Bird;
Remember her name is recorded
  On the pages of God's Holy Word.

Desiring to lower her standard,
  They watch every move that she makes;
They long to find fault with her teaching,
  But really they find no mistake.

I am glad I have learned of her meekness,
  I'm proud that my name is in the book;
For I want to be one never fearing
  The face of my Saviour's true looks.

When He cometh, descending from heaven
  On the clouds as He writes in His word,
I'll be joyfully carried to meet Him
  On the wings of the Great Speckled Bird.

—"The Great Speckled Bird"
(traditional)

Roy Acuff's Nashville

Prologue

Fiddle sounds and bluetick hounds and the smell of country ham in an iron skillet, and the soft haze of the Great Smoky Mountains.

More than anything else, I remember the sounds of early morning; those clean, crisp, cheery sounds that were so distinguishable: The snap of a poplar branch and the thump of Papa's rubber-soled work shoe as it broke through the stick and hit the floor. Another snap. And another. Then the high-pitched squeak of the cast-iron door on the patched-up old Burnside stove.

I suppose the pleasantness wasn't so much the *sounds* of the kindling being sized to fit in the stove's pot belly, or even the crackling of the blaze that followed; it was knowing that within minutes the flames would begin to take away the winter bite from the linoleum floor. There's nothing that gets your attention any quicker than bare feet on cold linoleum. So every morning, I would pull the covers up tight under my chin and wait for the East Tennessee dawn. And I would listen to a soft fiddle coming from the kitchen.

Every morning was the same, and I don't mind to admit that there are times when I still lie in bed and listen. Oh, how I would love to hear my father breaking up branches and playing the fiddle, waiting for the sun to come up so we could feed. There's no feeding to be done anymore. I'm going to be eighty soon and I guess the one thing that puzzles me most is how quick it got here. It just doesn't seem that long since those early years in Maynardville. Those morning memories of the fire and of my father's fiddle are still right there in the front of my memory.

I can see him lifting the fiddle to his shoulder and softly and delicately carving out "Wildwood Flower" or "When the Roll Is Called Up Yonder" or "Maple on the Hill," just like it was last week or maybe last year. He may not have been the best fiddler around, but to a little kid in Tennessee, he was all I ever needed to look up to. He was a fine Christian gentleman.

In fact, my whole family and my upbringing and the home were all anybody would have needed. Besides my mother and father, there was Briscoe, Juanita, Sue and Claude, who we called "Spot" because of his freckles. And the house was just a little old three-room cottage—well, not really a cottage, more of a shack, I suppose, but it was a special shack.

And mornings aren't the only fond times I can remember. There was a *lot* of magic to the period. I can remember lying in my bed at night and listening to the dogs up there on the hill, running a fox. The sound of a bluetick hound baying is something you can't describe. If you haven't heard that deep, swelling voice of a fox hound, then you've missed something. It sounds like, well, maybe like it was coming from a barrel. Or a cave. If you're ever down in the hills late at night, listen. Everybody should hear it once.

I can remember sitting on the porch with my family at night, and listening to a mixture of sounds: a fiddle or a guitar here and there; a gramophone down the dirt street, playing Enrico Caruso (it was always Caruso and always the same song, night after night); and kids playing hide-and-seek. Small-town sounds never change. Somehow they are more pure and more simple than any others. It's almost like they have been distilled down to a very *basic* sound.

That's how I recall my childhood: fiddle sounds and bluetick hounds and the smell of country ham in an iron skillet, and the soft haze of the Great Smoky Mountains. It was just beautiful. Any other recollections aren't really that important. Besides, they've all been written before, by everybody who grew up in the Southern mountains around the turn of the century.

Oh, I want to touch on some of the high spots of my early life, but I want to get to the music days as quick as I can, because, after all, this book will be more about *all of us* who grew up and learned to play country music, and about how and why this wonderful form of music got to where it is today. It wasn't an easy climb for any of us—or for the music itself, for that matter—but then living through a couple of wars and a depression wasn't easy either. And I'll be the first to admit that country music, more often that not, dwells on the struggles.

I've always heard that country music is one of our only true art forms. Maybe so, but to me it's a lot simpler than that: It's the music of our people and our places. Maybe it does have folk or soul leanings, but to me, it's just country—hillbilly if you wish, and I don't mind that because *I* am and *it* is. Anybody who tries to make much more than that out of it is just making it far too fancy and too complicated.

1

Come spring of 1930, I planned to be in the pinstripes of the New York Yankees.

When anybody moved in those days—even if it was only a few miles—it was a major undertaking. And it always looked like something right out of a John Steinbeck novel. So in 1919 when Papa borrowed Maynardville's only automobile for our move to Fountain City, it was no exception. To begin with, piling five kids and Mama and Papa into the 1917 Hupmobile was a task. There were arms and legs and cardboard suitcases and pasteboard boxes everywhere. And there was everything strapped on the car, from an old wooden folding ironing board to boxes of Papa's law books.

Nobody moved furniture because nobody *owned* furniture. It always came with the rented houses. Somebody had to own the houses and furniture, but I can't remember anybody *I* knew owning much of anything. But, for one reason or another, people moved a lot. We were no different.

In addition to being a lawyer, Papa was a Baptist minister, and he had wanted to move nearer Knoxville because the schools were better. I had gone as far as I could go in Maynardville, finishing the Big Room, which was for the fifth through eighth grades. Spot had finished the Little Room.

We never had much money, just like everybody else around us, and it was ten years before terms like "depression" and "poverty" came along; and it was at least a generation or two before anybody even *knew* they lived in "Appalachie." Or cared. We all accepted what we had, and even though it was precious little, it was adequate. There simply wasn't much one could have had if one had wanted it. Everybody had one dress-up outfit and some work clothes and, if one was lucky, a fiddle or a guitar. That took care of everything from work to church to entertainment. Enough to keep a man's soul in order.

Nobody got spoiled.

Radio came along in 1920. I remember reading about station KDKA in Pittsburgh in the newspapers but since that was light-years away, nobody even had a radio. And phonographs—gramophones, we called them—were about as scarce as automobiles. When we visited somebody, say, from Papa's congregation who had a gramophone, they usually had a couple of Caruso records. I thought for years that Enrico Caruso was the only person in the world who made records. And I didn't like his music half as much as what I heard in church or at hoedowns.

The music that really pleased me was the breakdown fiddle and the guitar music of the hills and the gospel music of the church. It was easy to listen to and easy to sing. And up until the time we moved to Fountain City, that's about the only contact I had with the outside world.

Central High School brought me sports, and I played everything. I was small, so I had to depend on my speed and on quick moves. I could also depend on maturity, since I was eighteen when I entered high school. But most of my teammates were nearly as old as I, and a lot of them had been playing for years. You see, eligibility was something else that hadn't yet come into vogue. So our high school teams looked a lot like college teams do today.

I practiced longer and harder than most of the boys (men?) because I had this strong feeling inside that made me want to excel. I suppose it's that way with a lot of smaller people. It may be why I loved to fight.

I couldn't begin to count the number of fights I got into. I also can't remember losing one. My fighting style was the same as my football and baseball technique. I was quick. I always had this philosophy: If you see you're going to have a fight—if it's just so obvious that it can't be avoided—walk right up, smiling, and pop him about four or five quick ones, and it's usually all over. It didn't matter how big the other guy was, he was whipped, even if he got up.

After I graduated from high school in 1924, I spent the next couple of years loafing around. Oh, I would pick up a job here and there, but nothing very serious. I spent more time hanging around Sherman Wallace's barbershop than anything else. I helped an old black fellow named Charley Duncan shine shoes.

Charley and I used to try to outdo each other with the "rhythm of the rag." He'd pop that rag and sing a chorus or two of some hillbilly song, then I'd do the same thing. I always had a little more rhythm than he did, but somehow his shoeshines were better than mine. I got so carried away with the beat and with the song that most of the time my rag didn't even touch the shoes. But it sure sounded good. More than once I heard: "Nice song, Roy. Now how 'bout runnin' through it again. And this time, hit the shoes."

Somehow I just couldn't get into working.

I played a lot of semi-pro baseball, and I listened to a lot of music. *Those* were my interests, in that order. For one thing, I had discovered records. I mean, *real* records. Music like Vernon Dalhart, who had a couple of good country records—hits of the time, I suppose, although I didn't know what a "hit" was then. There were songs like "The Little Old Cabin in the Lane" and "The Old Hen Cackled and the Rooster's Going to Crow." Vernon Dalhart sang in an untrained voice, but he played the fiddle at the same time, and that amazed me. Then there were the Skillet Lickers (Gid Tanner, Riley Puckett and Clayton McMichen) with "Alabama Jubilee," which was one of my favorites. Fiddlin' John Carson had "The Wreck of the Old 97" and "Prisoner's Song," and I remember Uncle Dave Macon's "Fox Hunt" and "Hill Billie Blues."

The fever had started. For me, at least. Radio still was a novelty in the mid-twenties. A few crystal sets began to appear, and I can remember ads in the newspapers where you could send away for a crystal set that you could build for a couple of dollars that would bring in stations "from miles and miles away." The only trouble was, there weren't many stations for us.

Radio was to come to us a few years later when WNOX and WROL opened stations in Knoxville. Needless to say, they were country music stations. Nobody would have listened to anything else anyway.

Toward the end of the twenties we all pitched in and got Mama a radio. It was a table-model Zenith and it was a delight. For all of us. We would turn it on and wait for what seemed an eternity for it to warm up, and then we would turn through all the static until we got a station clear enough to listen to. Then we would all gather around the set and listen to every word. To say that it provided hours of entertainment would be a great understatement. Not only did it broaden my scope of musical artists, but I also began to learn new songs.

I heard a lot of talk about Jimmie Rodgers, so I listened to his records every chance I got. His recordings of "Sleep, Baby Sleep," "Soldier's Sweetheart," "Lonely and Blue," and all the "Blue Yodel" songs impressed me no end. I'm sure Jimmie Rodgers somehow influenced me even then, just as he had to influence nearly every country music artist who was around at that time. He had a wonderful, sincere voice, and I wondered how a person ever got good enough to make a record like that.

I listened to his records whenever I could, and there were

many times when I just sat and looked at those old, thick Victor records and tried to imagine how it felt to play and sing like that. But it was hard for me to imagine because I didn't play any instrument at all and the only singing I had done was either in church or in school, hardly show business. I had done some acting in high school and it felt good to be up there in front of everybody, but as for performing, I always figured I'd leave that to the baseball diamond.

In 1929 it appeared that I would have a chance. Some scouts for the New York Yankees came through Knoxville in the spring and, after a tryout, they invited me to their training camp the following spring. I was walking on air.

I had a job with the Louisville and Nashville Railroad as a callboy (I rounded up train crews and gave orders to the various trains as to where they were to go), but, like most of my jobs, I looked at it as temporary because, come spring of 1930, I planned to be in the pinstripes of the New York Yankees. The job did give me enough money to buy a brand-new Chevrolet sports roadster with wire wheels and a rumble seat. It was red, which fit my image pretty well. I was doing a whole lot of carousing with the boys; so much that I spent a few nights in jail. It's a good thing my father was a lawyer. My fists were improving my image as a lightweight, but they weren't doing much for his as a preacher.

Papa preached a good sermon—fortunately for me, he was good in front of a jury, too—but he didn't spend a whole lot of time preaching to me. When he did give me advice, I tried to listen, because I knew he meant it. But when he came to me after one of my brushes with the law and put his arm around my shoulders, I knew it was father-and-son talk time. I would have been a lot better off if I had listened to him sooner, and I've always been sorry that he wasn't around in later years when I had made a name for myself, just to let him see that his advice finally took hold.

But this time I didn't listen too well, I guess. He said, "Roy, your mother and I are worried about you. I mean, we're proud of all of our children, but you, Roy, you've got more of what it takes to be a leader than any of them. And what you're doing, well, it's reflecting on all of us."

Then, in his best courtroom voice, he said: "Roy, if you don't shape up and stop drinking and carousing, you're apt to wind up in prison."

I thought about what he had said, and then I answered him as honestly as I could: "Well, Papa, I can't think of a thing I'd rather go to prison for than drinking and carousing."

In spite of his strict Christian beliefs, I could tell he was fighting back a smile. So was Mama. End of father-and-son talks.

I often wonder how my life would have turned out if I had become a pitcher for the Yankees. Most people never even knew I had a chance because, well, I never *got* the chance.

My Central High School yearbook picture. (Roy Acuff Collection)

The Life and Good Times of Country Music

That magic spring of 1930 that was to catapult me into the limelight as a professional athlete passed me by.

In the summer of 1929 I went on a fishing trip to Soldier Key in Florida with a friend, Ross Smith. Having grown up in the mountains where it never got all that hot—even in playing baseball for years, where you spend half an inning in the sun and half in the dugout—I had never been exposed to sun like we found in the Florida Keys, with the rays magnified from all sides by the water and white sand. I blistered so badly that I had to sit up all night to sleep. I couldn't wear a shirt, and the pain was so bad that I had to move like a robot. But the pain went away in a few days, and I pronounced myself well enough to play ball.

Wrong. About two innings into my next baseball game, I began to feel weak. My curve ball wasn't working and my fastball got slower with each pitch. Each time I reached down to get some dirt on my fingertips, I came up with mud. There was no sweat anywhere else, just on my hands. I tried to focus on the signal from the catcher, but the ground began to rock back and forth like the Florida surf. I told the manager I wanted to be taken off the mound, so he moved me to the outfield. At the end of the fourth inning, I ran in from right field and promptly collapsed in the dugout. My arms and legs cramped so much it took four teammates to straighten me out.

Later, at the hospital, the doctor told me that the severe sunburn had damaged the pores of my skin so badly that the palms of my hands were the only places on my upper torso where any perspiration could come out. As a result, I had suffered sunstroke on the diamond.

A week later, I passed out again when I tried to get out of bed. The doctor then told me that I must get back in bed and stay there—for maybe a year—if I expected to live.

Nobody had to tell me that my days as an athlete were over. For day after endless day, I lay in bed and wondered what it was I had to live for anyway.

If there was anything that got me through those first weeks, it was Mama's Zenith radio. I discovered the Carter Family and got to know more about Jimmie Rodgers's music. But, more important, I discovered something that would eventually change my entire life. I began to live for Saturday nights, because it was then that I listened to the Grand Ole Opry. All the way from Nashville.

2

The blues ain't nothin' but a good man feelin' bad.

—*"Hard Time Blues"*
by Jimmie Rodgers

We had an old time-Victrola, the kind where the whole top opened up to expose the turntable and the big, round head that swung back so you could change the needle, which you had to do after twenty or so plays. A little paper package of needles cost a dime and we always had a good supply. There was a hand crank on the right side of the white oak cabinet and double doors in front with brown burlap-looking cloth behind cut-out wooden cathedral arch designs. It stood on tall legs, and the whole thing was about four feet high.

Behind the doors was the record cabinet, with Papa's collection of old fiddle songs. I listened to them by the hour. Eventually, of course, I picked up Papa's fiddle and tried to pick out some of the songs by ear. But it was difficult for me to even tell what key they were in because the speed of the record changed as the Victrola ran down. I would always have to stop playing to wind it up. There were times when the records sounded real bad. But, even at worst, they sounded better than my playing.

The effects of my therapy must have been costly to everybody's eardrums, but they never said a word. I guess they could tell that I was in a different world when I had that fiddle tucked under my chin. A man named Al Cassidy from May-nardville had hand-carved the fiddle in 1907, and though I have owned many fiddles since then, I loved that one the most.

I spent hours each day sawing away at all the traditional music of the hills. And I would sing along, but that never seemed too important to me, because everybody could sing. We sang at church and at social functions and every time we got the chance. It was just the natural thing to do. But not everybody could play an instrument, so that became an obsession with me. Papa was the first to realize this and he began to take more and more time with me, lovingly showing me everything he knew about the fiddle. And my uncle Charlie, who was a pretty good country fiddler in his own right, would come by and help me.

While I was fiddling, my sister Sue was practicing her voice exercises. She was taking lesons to be a really serious singer, and as she ran the scales and did all the things her voice teacher had told her to practice, I would lay down the fiddle and trill my voice just like hers. It sounded a whole lot like a dog baying at the moon, but I would wail away in a comic-opera falsetto voice and she would finally run from the house bawling. I didn't even have to look around because I could *feel* Mama standing behind me with her hands on her hips. I would sheepishly pick up the fiddle and start playing away.

You know, I think it was this teasing of Sue that taught me to really develop my voice. Completely by accident, I learned to sing from the pit of my stomach instead of with the nose-and-mouth tones I had sung before. There's no question that it made me different from most of the country singers I had been listening to on the radio and on records. It gave me a much stronger voice, although it didn't do much for Sue's career as a serious singer.

About the time the whole family's sanity was at the breaking point, I discovered John Copeland's garage. It was nothing but a big old two-story frame building, but my daily walks past the place revealed some interesting sounds—not the sounds of a mechanic but the strains of some pretty good old-time country music. I found out that, in addition to being a mechanic and a fox-hunter without peer, John Copeland was a fair-to-middlin' country fiddler.

I made the garage a daily stop. Sometimes twice daily. It was a prescription no doctor could have bettered.

John was a free-style character who often slept in the car with his dogs, and he talked to them just like they were human. He had a big, bushy beard and he wore the same pair of bib overalls every day. He may well have been the world's first hippie. But he became a good friend and every time I stopped by, he slid out from under the car he was working on or put down the carburetor he was rebuilding and sat down to talk. John didn't get much mechanicking done, but we got a lot of country music talk in as we sat on the nail kegs around the battered Burnside stove.

John sawed away on his fiddle, and he told stories while he played. If he played "Sally Goodin," there was a story that went with that tune; if he played "Wildwood Flower," there was one for that one. The stories never varied, and they always began the same way: "When I was a lad . . ." And then he would proceed to tell me how, when he was a lad, the first time he ever heard that particular song he was playing something exciting and fascinating happened to him. John had done more and knew more people than any man I had ever met. Now that I look back on it, that's still true. If even a fraction of the stories John told were true, he would have to have been two hundred years old at the time I was going in there.

I started taking my fiddle in to John's garage and we sat by the hour and played and told stories. John and I played and I listened to the stories. The only break we had was when some irate customer came in to find out why his car was two days late in getting fixed.

But life was a whole lot simpler in those days. There was an easygoing pace to life—at least in our neck of the woods—and people didn't get too upset about things like not having a car to drive for a couple of days. Just as often as not, the guy who came in fuming ended up sitting down and listening to us play. And more than once, he pulled a guitar or a banjo out of the backseat of the car and joined right in.

I don't know if it was because there were more people who played music in those days or if word just got around town, but more and more people started showing up with musical instruments tucked under their arms. We began to have some real sessions. It wasn't unusual to have four or five people playing away at John's garage. And the sounds attracted an audience. You see, there just weren't that many cars in those days and people walked more than they drove, so there was a lot of "stoppin' in." It took a long time to walk, say, from one of the houses on State Street down to the corner grocery store, because there were regular "stop in" places along the route. People took time to stop and sit down and talk. For one thing, it was the only way they had of finding out what was going on in the neighborhood. They didn't much care what was happening on the other side of the Clinch Mountains, they were more interested in who was doing what in their own community.

Like I said, it was a simpler time. People around us were a lot more important than those in some far-off land like Iran or Cambodia. And the only soap operas we knew anything about were the ones we were living.

At the garage, we played away for our audience, which sometimes was as big as eight or ten people, and then we stopped and chatted. You might have called a lot of the talk "gossip," but we thought of it as, well, as spreading the news. John Copeland's place became a cross between the local music hall and the daily newspaper, with an occasional auto repair job thrown in. But only an occasional one. John didn't let work get in the way of his pleasure too often.

There's no question in my mind that we could have put on some real shows if we had put our minds to it; I mean, shows where you got up on the stage and charged money. Those kind of shows. But getting paid for playing music never occurred to any of us. Music was something that was so natural to people around there that you just did it because you loved it. You didn't get paid for it.

Whatever "itch to pitch" I had was taken up with the yo-yo. I substituted it for the desire that lingered to play ball. And I became pretty good at it. It was about the only time I didn't have a fiddle or a fork in my hand, because playing the fiddle and eating were my only pastimes. That and the Grand Ole Opry.

To say I had become an Opry fan would be putting it mildly. All week long I waited for Saturday night so I could tune in WSM and listen to the Solemn Old Judge, George D. Hay, and Sam and Kirk McGee and Uncle Dave Macon and the steady stream of performers who became my personal friends via the Zenith speaker.

I noticed that the music was starting to change in the thirties. Much of the music we called mountain or hillbilly was a combination of the traditional Scottish-Irish ballads and songs the singers created from their own experiences. I suppose this is why a lot of people insist on putting country music in the same category as folk music. If it is, it's the folk music of the Southern hills. And it was interesting to hear the effects of the Negro on the music of the Southern lowlands, and of the Cajun on Louisiana music, not to mention the Mexican influence on Western music.

It was all beginning to change by, say, 1931. The one thing that wasn't changing that fast, though, was the breakdown fiddle. It was still the basic instrument. The guitar still remained popular, but more and more bands were adding

The Delmore Brothers, Rabon (left) and Alton (right), join Uncle Dave Macon on an early WSM radio broadcast. (From the collection of Les Leverett)

Country music groups get together to play any time there was more than one instrument between them. The Crook Brothers, here, were one of the first groups to appear on the Grand Ole Opry. From left to right: Herman Crook, Lewis Crook, Blythe Poteet, Kirk McGee and Bill Stone. (From the collection of Les Leverett)

string bass and, in our area and on the Opry, the five-string banjo. Occasionally a mandolin crept in. But the musical structure was pretty much the same no matter what instruments there were: the fiddle was the lead, with the guitar and string bass carrying the rhythm. The role of singer hadn't yet made its appearance, so different members of the bands would sing when the time was appropriate.

But the music still wasn't all that respectable. Why, you couldn't even get into a country club if you were a country musician. It was a time when, if you walked down the street with a fiddle or guitar in your hand, some people would snicker. "There's one now. He just got in," they would say. And we were classified as *hillbillies,* which is not all that bad if you consider that living in the hills was probably a better life than any of them were used to in the city. I, for one, am proud of it.

The term hillbilly got started during World War I, or so the story goes. It seems that so many of the boys from Tennessee and Virginia and West Virginia were called Billy, that people got to saying, "Here comes another one of those Billys from the hills. Damn hillbillies."

Probably the only person associated with country music at that time that wasn't thought of as a "hillbilly" was Jimmie Rodgers. In some way, this reflected the enormous talent of the "Singing Brakeman."

The most touching story I ever heard about him was that of his last days. It is a scene of a dying man, resting on a cot in RCA's New York recording studio, trying to gain strength to cut the next song. It was truly the last-gasp effort of a dedicated musician trying to finish an album of the music he loved.

It was 1933 and Jimmie had become the brightest star of country music. He was making one hundred thousand dollars a year, but he was living a life of pain from tuberculosis, which he called "that ol' TB." Many of the musicians that I talked to thought of Jimmie as the father of the country music we knew by then, or they referred to him as "the man who started it all," And I think they were right on both counts. Why; I'll bet he caused the sale of more phonographs and more guitars, and inspired more people to take up singing, than anyone who ever lived.

The story was that Jimmie was born to a railroad family and that it actually was Negroes on the line that taught him how to play the banjo and the guitar. I guess the singing and yodeling came naturally. And there's no question that he combined the best from the white and black musical heritages.

He had contracted tuberculosis in his twenties, which wasn't all that uncommon at that time, particularly among railroadmen. It forced him to give up railroading, and though it was tragic, if it hadn't been for that "ol' TB," the world might never have had the opportunity to hear the "Blue Yodeler." Moneyless, he turned to music in 1927 to make a living. And it's fortunate, because he did well.

He recorded hit song after hit song about railroads and gamblers and cowboys and hoboes and convicts—songs like "Hobo's Meditation," "Take Me Back Again," "Ninety-Nine Year Blues," "In the Jailhouse Now," "I'm Lonely and Blue," "A Drunkard's Child," "Whippin' That Ol' TB," "Yodelin' My Way Back Home," "Train Whistle Blues," "Any Old Time," and "Yesterday."

Jimmie Rodgers stood as a symbol to millions who also suffered, not from the physical pain he did, but from hunger and poverty. There were stories of people who went to town to buy a small sack of groceries and a Jimmie Rodgers rocord. I guess it was his singing and his spirit that got a lot of them through the depression years.

The world—and certainly me included—couldn't imagine the little man with the big bow tie and the straw hat not being around to sing anymore, but he was dying. The "Blue Yodeler" was one of the few bright spots in a depression-torn land. Perhaps it was this overall atmosphere of sadness that

Jimmie Rodgers, the "Singing Brakeman." (From the collection of Les Leverett)

contributed to the saga of the skinny little man from Mississippi. I remember so well listening to one of his songs, "No Hard Times," and thinking how hard he was trying to cheer everyone up, and to let them know that there was a bright spot down the road. I still think of those words:

> *I got a barrel of flour, Lord I got a bucket of lard*
> *I ain't got no blues, got chickens in my yard.*
> *Got corn in my crib, cotton growin' in my patch*
> *Got that old hen settin, waitin' for that old hen to hatch.*
>
> *Gonna' buy all my chillin a brand new pair of shoes*
> *I'm gonna' quit singin' these dog-gone hard time blues.*

Jimmie Rodgers died at the age of thirty-five. He didn't finish that last recording session.

3

*Bob Wills and Gene Autry and Red Skelton
got started in medicine shows, so if it was
good enough for them . . .*

I suppose the first stage I really had was our front porch. It
ran all across the front of the house and halfway down the
side to where the front door was. Center stage was an old
hickory swing with a bottom of woven wooden strips. Swings
like that were popular in the thirties because they added a
rustic touch and they lasted for years. Besides that, they were
cheap.

The swing was in front of a big double-width parlor window, and I sat there by the hour, sawing away at the fiddle
and singing. It was also the finest vantage point for most
everything that was going on in Fountain City. What didn't
happen right before my eyes was told to me by the parade of
people who happened by. Most of them stopped to talk. I
became the unofficial chronicler of the community because,
well, because I was *available*. It was the TV news of an earlier
time.

I've noticed that people will tell you about almost anything
if you just sit and listen. But a lot of the people made regular
rounds to listen to my music; I'm glad because I don't think I
would have gone on if I hadn't had some kind of regular
audience, even though it was a one-at-a-time audience. I've
seen it many times since; a true performer will put on just as

good a show for an audience of three as he will for three thousand. It's what separates the *performer* from the *players*.

I had a feeling that I was starting to become a performer because I could really feel a difference in my playing when there was somebody out there beyond the banister from when I was alone. Oh, most of the time, I played for myself. There weren't that many people who stopped. Just regulars, I guess, but it seemed like a lot. I picked out songs that I had heard on the radio broadcasts of the Opry or from records or the impromptu shows at John Copeland's garage and I lived for the times when somebody stopped and said, "Lemme hear what you've got new for me, Roy."

Well, with this I would rear back, stuff that fiddle deep under my chin and really put my heart into it. I sat there and played—eyes closed and truly mesmerizing *myself*—for as long as the person would stay. You have no idea how much I felt that porch was a stage. I was up there, say, three feet higher than the "audience" and the whole world was mine.

I played the "porch circuit" for about a year, and if nothing else, it gave me some sort of a feeling for the real stage. It also provided me with a whale of a repertoire, because I had to learn new and different songs for my regulars. I weeded out the ones people didn't seem to like, and moved the more popular ones up in the "act." I mean, if John Fowler said he thought "Wildwood Flower" was the best thing I did, I played that all day long, for everybody who stopped. And, in my unofficial popularity poll, if enough people said kind things about it, it became part of the act.

And if Aunt Sara Jean or Miz Wilson said they thought "Banks of the Ohio" or "Only One Step More" or "There'll Come a Time" were "just lovely, Roy," well, you can bet they stayed in. I was building an act out there in the stars for me.

I had moved from the back porch when I felt I was good enough for some more people to hear, so it was as natural as the flowers for me to think that I would move on to something better. And not just another porch. A real stage, with real people paying real money to listen to me. I've never been a negative-thinking person.

And, you know, the fateful day that I was to move from the porch to the real world of show business wasn't all that long in coming. It wasn't exactly the Opry, but it sure was going to be a good start.

Doc Hauer was a Knoxville doctor. Now that I think of it, I'm not sure he was even a doctor at all. In fact, I'm sure he *wasn't,* but he concocted all types of patent medicines and everybody called him *Doctor* Hauer or just "Doc." There were people all over town that swore by his medicine, and I had heard about it since we moved from Maynardville. Well, Doc had become one of my regular customers. He would come by, pull up one of the straight-backed chairs on the porch and listen to me play and sing, just leaning back against the clapboard siding on two chair legs and listening.

"Roy," he said one day, "I'm puttin' together this medicine show and we're gonna travel all over the country. I mean, son, we're gonna see some of that land out there," and he drew a big arch in the air with his big ham hand, indicating the land beyond the Clinch Mountains. It had always been my dream just to get beyond those mountains. I really didn't care where, just out there in that land that Doc referred to.

He put his arm around my shoulder. "And, Roy," he continued, in an almost mystical tone, "I'm gonna take you with me. You're gonna play those tunes for the world, son, you're gonna play 'em, why in North Carolina and West Virginny and maybe even Ohi'a, Roy. Just think, *Ohi'a.*"

The bow skipped down the strings as I stopped playing. I raised my chin and looked at him. "Ohi'a." He meant it. He *was* asking me to go with the medicine show.

"You see, Roy, I got this idea," he said. "Why, we're gonna hit all those towns and you and a couple other boys'll sing and play and there'll be all those crowds. And they'll love ya, son.

They'll love ya." He was up on his feet, gesturing wildly by now.

"Then we'll sell Mocoton Tonic. Man, I'll tell you we'll sell Mocoton. Why, they'll be fighting to buy it. And, you know what? You'll make some money." He took me by the shoulders and he shook me just once and looked straight into my eyes. "Some real money," he said.

Mocoton Tonic was one of Doc's patent medicines. I had heard a lot of people say it really worked, just like he said, for everything from headaches to hangnails.

What a thought! Show business!

Then my heart sank because I knew I couldn't do it. He was still holding me by the shoulders, and his head was moving up and down slightly, like he was waiting for an answer. What came out of my mouth, I couldn't even believe.

"Doc," I said, "that's probably the best thing anybody ever said to me. I mean, the *best,* 'cause there's nothing I'd rather do than play. I mean, play for people, lots of people, but, you see, well . . . aw, hell, Doc, I can't do it."

"Whattaya mean, you can't do it?" he asked in amazement.

"Well, you see, the only reason I'm out here on this porch every day is because of the sunstroke. Even Mocoton Tonic can't cure that. I just can't be out in the sun, Doc."

My heart was broken. I just stood there, looking at the floor, with my arms down at my sides, the fiddle in one hand and the bow in the other. Doc still had me by the shoulders, and he shook me once more.

"Listen, son," he said in a sincere, fatherly tone, "We'll keep you in the shade all the time. Besides, most of the shows are at night. You can do it if you *want* to."

"If I want to," I thought to myself. "If I *want* to."

I thought of how many people had gotten their starts in medicine shows. Bob Wills and Gene Autry and Red Skelton had played them, and I figured that if it was good enough for them . . . well, you know the rest.

I looked him right in the eye. "Doc, you got yourself a fiddle player. When do we leave?"

Medicine shows were probably closer to the New York stage than they were to the Grand Ole Opry stage. It was 1932 and vaudeville had already started to fade out, giving way to motion pictures, so these medicine shows—and there were a lot of them traveling throughout the country, mostly the South and Southwest—sort of filled the gap. In fact, most of the towns the shows played never would have attracted vaudeville in the first place.

I'll never forget the day Doc came to pick me up. The 1930 REO Flying Cloud sedan was all washed up and shining like a silver dollar. He had cut the back out of the car—the part that had been the trunk—and there was a sort of wooden platform that would fit onto the car, so that it could be used as a stage for small crowds. For larger audiences, a separate truck with a flat bed was used. This gave the medicine show group a real stage to work on. But when that REO with the fender-mounted spare tires rolled up, I was as nervous as a cat.

The other two members of the "show" were already in the car. Jack Tindell, the guitarist, was in the front seat, and Clarence Ashley, who played banjo and guitar, was in the back.

I had gotten a lot of encouragement from all my family. They were all there to see me off. My father put his arm around me and said, "Roy, if I was your age, I'd be doing the same thing as you're about to do." It meant a lot to me. I was ready to conquer that world out there beyond the mountains.

"Hop in, Roy," Doc said. "It's gonna be everything you hoped it would."

Our first trip wasn't exactly *beyond* the mountains. In fact, it was only twenty-five miles away in Maryville, but as Papa told me, "a journey of a thousand miles starts with a single step." That was my single step.

We got to where Doc wanted to "set up" at about three o'clock in the afternoon and he, as good as his word, said "Roy, I'll park the car in the shade over here and you just stay out of the sun. I'm gonna put up a few signs and talk to a few people, just to get the word out that we'll be puttin' on a show tonight. We'll work off the back of the car tonight, and when word gets out, we'll need the big stage for tomorrow and the next few days."

It was Doc's practice—and I was later to find out that it was a pretty general tent show practice—to stay in one town for a week or ten days. In that length of time, I'll guarantee you, everybody who could possibly have been persuaded to buy some of the patent medicine had bought it.

I sat there in the car and I read the label on one of the bottles of Mocoton: "Cures dyspepsia, sick headaches, constipation, indigestion, pain in the side, back and limbs, torpid liver, etc.; ten percent alcohol." I was to learn that that "etc." would cover everything else.

The other two performers were veterans of the traveling circuit. Jake Tindell had been with Doc for years, and Clarence Ashley had been in the medicine show business in general for twenty years. And when he wasn't on a stage somewhere, Clarence was playing the streets or at carnivals or fairs.

There were people like Jake and Clarence all over the South, and the historians who like to think of radio as being the proving grounds for country performers are wrong. The medicine show went back years before radio ever existed. It was the vaudeville of America's South, at least the small towns and hamlets of the South. Playing the streets was as accepted as the music itself.

As I sat there under a big old oak tree, Jake gave me my first stage lesson. He told me a few jokes that I could use, and filled me in on a couple of the skits we would probably use later on. We also went over most of the songs that *they* used. He was impressed that I knew so many songs. What he didn't realize was that I had spent two long years' apprenticeship in John Copeland's garage and on my own front porch. You learn a lot of songs that way.

Doc came back in a couple of hours. "Well, boys, we're gonna put on a show at seven o'clock," he said. "Everybody'll be finished with supper by then, and I figure we can draw maybe four, five hundred people."

Doc had been doing the medicine show for a long time and he knew exactly who to talk to in every town—the people would go out and get the word around that there would be a free show tonight. And it was always a free show. In fact, the whole thing was sort of like a gypsy troupe. Here would come this old car full of musicians and boxes of patent medicine, and they would set up some kind of stage and start playing. People would just appear, or so Doc said, as if by magic.

And he proved it.

Doc backed up the REO right near the edge of the vacant lot, which was about a block and a half from the main part of town. There was a small grove of trees at the edge of the lot and he put the nose of the car right in the trees. It gave us a big open arena to play to.

"This'll be a good spot for all week, Roy," he said. "You see, we'll get the truck here tomorrow and we'll all set up the big stage and, lemme tell you, son, we'll be in *business*. You'll get a taste of what it's like to have a whole sea of people out there, cheerin' and hollerin' for you." And he spread his hand across the whole area. I could see them all out there, cheering and waving. Doc gestured a lot with his hands and I gobbled it all up.

And sure enough, people began to trickle in. A couple from up the street, and then four or five more and, as the crowd started to grow, people would stop and park their cars and get out to see what was going on. Jake looked over at me and said, "Tune up, Roy, the fun's about to start."

When the instruments came out, the crowd, which by now was probably a hundred people, seemed to get into the swing of things. Doc climbed up on the small wooden platform on the back of the REO and he said, "Ladies and gentlemen and children alike, the show's ready to begin. You're gonna hear some good old down-home music and some gospel songs and the boys and me are going to tell you a few jokes and I guarantee you, you're gonna have a good time. And I'll guarantee you one more thing, you're gonna see a *family* show. You'll never see or hear a thing in one of Doc Hauer's shows that you wouldn't go home and tell your dear ol' grandma."

And then he motioned to us to come over near the platform.

"Ladies and gentlemen and children alike, here's Jake Tindell on guitar and Clarence Ashley on banjo and Roy Acuff on fiddle. It's the famous Doc Hauer Medicine Show, and we're gonna be here to enter*tain* you all week. Bring your friends and the rest of your families tomorrow night. Come on up, boys."

Doc stepped down and we climbed up. I looked out over the hundred or so people, and for a second or two I thought I was going to pass out. I had a knot in my stomach and my throat was as dry as a corncob. My palms were sweating and I had this pounding in my head. I leaned over to Jake and said, "Jake, I'm not sure I can . . ." But it was too late. Doc yelled out, "How 'bout 'Are You From Dixie,' boys? Just to get things rollin'."

Jake looked at me and said, "You're gonna do fine, Roy," and he hit a chord on the guitar. I don't even remember putting the fiddle to my shoulder, but before I knew it we were right into "Are You From Dixie." The pounding in my head had stopped and the knot was gone from my stomach. Man, I was in show business.

I probably learned more about show business in that first week than I did at any similar period in my entire life. And it was show business as much as anything anybody was doing. We were playing to crowds of up to three thousand people, who had come from miles around to see the shows. We worked on the stage, which was five or six feet above the audience. Doc had a format that worked so well I adopted it for my own shows in later years. He opened the show with a few welcoming remarks, then we would play four or five songs and Jake and I would do a comedy skit—which is another side of the business I never expected to be in. I remember the first one very clearly. I played a blackface comedian and I was Jake's straight man, which was right because most of the jokes were his. I found out that the laughter made me feel almost as good as the applause from playing the fiddle and singing.

Here's an example:

Jake: "Roy, that girl over there's about the ugliest girl I've ever seen."

Roy: "Aw, Jake, that's not nice. You know beauty is only skin deep."

Jake: "Well, then let's skin her."

It may not have been the best humor in the world, but it was free.

People were still laughing when Doc came to the stage. They thought he was going to join in with the frivolity. Man, were they wrong. He was moving into his Mocoton Tonic pitch. And the stories he would tell usually had people in tears. He would tell of worms devouring little children because they didn't have Mocoton. The stories were so real that many times his wife would ask him not to tell them because they frightened her. But he went right on.

While Doc was telling the stories, Jake and Clarence and I had already gone out into the audience with arms full of Mocoton Tonic. And then Doc would say, "Folks, you'll never have to live any of these tragic stories because the boys are down there amongst you right now, with a goodly supply of this wonderful elixir. So you just have your dollar bill ready and they'll let you have a bottle.

When we ran out, we yelled out at the top of our lungs,

"Hey, Doc, I'm sold out up here on Gobler's knob (or wherever we were), see if you can find some more for me," and we came back for another armload. We made so much fuss about running out that it looked like everybody was buying it. And every time we went back to get more, we got fewer bottles, so that it sold out faster.

Then we would sing some more songs and Doc would go into his corn remedy pitch. He would ask if there was anybody in the audience who was troubled by corns. There always was somebody who was more than willing to try anything. You see, people didn't have as many shoes as they do today, so they wore them much longer, and the shoes got hard and cracked and they rubbed your feet so much that it was bound to cause some kind of ache. Well, Doc would get some poor guy up there whose corns were about to kill him, and he would pour the medicine right on his shoe. "This where it is?" he would ask. "Yeah, Doc, right here." The medicine would soak right through the leather and into his foot. It had so much ether in it that it would actually numb not only the corn but the whole front part of his foot. Then Doc would put his shoe right on top of the afflicted area. "How's that feel, sir?" he would ask. And always the guy would say, "Great, Doc." Well, with that he would put his whole weight on the man's foot—and Doc was a big man—and the guy would just be all smiles. Talk about something that sold corn remedy medicine!

We sang some more songs and Doc would break out the homemade lye soap. What the Mocoton and the corn medicine wouldn't cure, the soap would wash away. We had a tub of water, to which we had added some liquid soap, so that when we put a washboard in it and scrubbed with the bar of Doc's soap, there would be suds everywhere.

The final sales pitch was for candy. There were coupons inside some of the wrappers and people could win some pretty nice prizes—blankets and flashlights and all sorts of things. Doc must have known which boxes had prizes in them, because the second or third one would always win something and we would yell out, "Over here, Doc. We've got a winner." Then you couldn't carry enough candy. Everything sold for a dollar.

We always ended the show—maybe two hours later—with what we called an "after piece," which was a little skit or play. I played everything from blackface to a little girl to an old man, but it was a nice ending. It left everybody well satisfied. That's why the crowds were so consistently big. Word would go out that there was this show over in Podunk for nothing—absolutely *nothing*—and they would come from all over. Well, the *show* was absolutely free, but if you could get away from one of Doc's sales pitches without buying something, then you were better than most. But, you know, I never heard a single complaint about any of his medicine.

And we did well, too. I was making about twenty dollars a week, sometimes thirty dollars, and that was big money in 1932. In fact, it was twenty or thirty dollars more than most people were making. And to think I was making it while doing something I really loved.

It was not only good experience for me, but I'm sure it's why I developed such a strong singing voice. We didn't have microphones, so to get across to two or three thousand people, you really had to project. It's also where I put to work what I had learned at Sue's expense. They heard me clear in the back row.

And I could feel the rhythm building as my voice developed more and more.

My biggest break came when Doc's brother died. I took over the pitches for him and found that I loved the number-one spot in the show more than anyplace else. I had heard the pitches so much that I could recite them word for word. I sold the tonic and corn medicine and soap and then I sold candy. I added one or two of my own gimmicks to the show.

From that day on, there was no turning back for me. Show business was what I wanted.

4

*Radio got a lot of people through the hard
times of the South . . . it helped
popularize country music.*

Radio in general and the Grand Ole Opry in particular got a whole lot of people through the depression. At least it made it a little easier for them. Oh, I'm sure they would have made it anyway, but it gave us all something to look forward to—Saturday night. And I don't mean going out and carousing Saturday night; I mean sitting home and listening to the radio Saturday night. The Opry wasn't the *only* Saturday night entertainment, but it was the most popular one in our neck of the woods.

People started getting ready for Saturday night when they got up on Saturday morning. They swept and dusted their parlors, made sure there were clean and freshly starched doilies on the arms of the mohair sofas—everybody had a mohair sofa—and they got the chairs all set in a semicircle around the radio; then they took baths, and the men slicked down their hair while the women curled theirs. The parlor was the most important room of the house on Saturday night, because that's where the radio was. You see, nobody, I mean *no*body had more than one radio, and it usually was such a big thing that the furniture was arranged around it, or, at least, so that everybody had a good place to sit. We all gathered around it like people do today with television, since it always was better, for some reason, if you were looking at it. You didn't carry the radio around like you do one of today's portables, you went to it. And you went to *listen*. It was an important item in everybody's home, and I don't care how poor you were, you found some way to own a radio. When the "wish books" came—the Sears and Roebuck or the Monkey Ward (Montgomery Ward) catalogs—the pages with the radios were the ones everybody turned to first.

Adults and kids alike were right there when the Opry started, and you didn't have to tell anybody to be quiet because everybody listened intently. Why, we even listened to

Dr. Humphrey Bate and his Possum Hunters were the first string band to appear on the Opry. They later adopted the more casual bib overall, straw hat, and work shoes costume that became a country music trademark. Dr. Bate, standing at left, was a prominent Tennessee surgeon who preferred the harmonica to the scalpel. (WSM Archives)

the commercials, and, if we could afford it, we bought the products they advertised. After all, they brought us the entertainment of the thirties.

A personal game that everybody played in those days was to connect faces and bodies to the voices of the singers and to the sounds of guitars and fiddles. It was one of the really nice things about radio; it made you use your imagination. But to me it was more than a game; it was, well, I guess you could call it research. I studied the styles of the musicians so that I could put together my own act. I mentally formed it from the medicine shows' format and from what I heard on radio. And, you know, I could just feel what it was like to be up there on the stage of the Grand Ole Opry in Nashville, which was, to me, the Carnegie Hall of country music. Radio was beckoning to me.

Saturday night wasn't the only radio time for country music. All over the country, there were morning and noontime shows and evening programs featuring country music. Both WROL and WNOX in Knoxville had early morning programs that featured live entertainment. They gave the weather and farm reports and played music and I don't suppose there was a farmer or anybody who got up early—I mean really early, say, five o'clock—who didn't have his radio turned to one or the other. When they came in from the field or wherever they came from for dinner, they listened to programs like the *Mid-Day Merry-Go-Round* on WNOX.

During those hard times in the South—the whole nation, for that matter—it was the only thing most people could afford to do. And there's no question, it helped to popularize country music. It carried "hillbilly" music far beyond the hills and into the living rooms of people everywhere, and turned it into "country" music.

It gave young musicians a tremendous opportunity, because there was so much country music programing that there weren't enough musicians to go around. It also was one of the reasons that country music got a sort of bad reputation at first, because some of it was bad. I'm sure that if you take any huge gathering of musicians—and I don't care if its hillbilly or classical—some of it is going to be good, most of it average and some of it bad. Well, the bad country music stood out like a sore thumb. The nasal, raspy singing and the off-key instrumentation grated on a lot of people's nerves. By the same token, when a really talented performer or group came along, they stood out just as clearly. It was one of the reasons for the instant popularity of people like Jimmie Rodgers and the Carter Family and Gene Autry.

Gene Autry, for example, became famous to a world of radio listeners long before he mounted Champion and rode across moving picture screens. Radio station WLS in Chicago (the call letters stood for "World's Largest Store"—Sears and Roebuck) went to fifty thousand watts, clear channel, just like WSM, which carried the Grand Ole Opry. We were able to pick up WLS on the Blue Network of the National Broadcasting Company. There was a great similarity between Gene's singing and that of Jimmie Rodgers, so he sort of filled an important void left by Jimmie's death.

The fact that Gene was also a good songwriter made him an early favorite of mine. I still marvel at the list of great songs that he wrote over the years, the most successful of which was "That Silver-Haired Daddy of Mine."

But there were scores of other songs he performed that were classics written by a lot of other songwriters. He was a true performer, and who can forget his renditions of songs like "Have I Stayed Away Too Long?" "Buttons and Bows," "Empty Cot in the Bunkhouse," "Mexacali Rose," "Back in the Saddle Again," "Yellow Rose of Texas," "Tumbling Tumbleweeds," "Have I Told You Lately That I Love You?" "Be Honest With Me," "Goodbye Little Darling," "You're the Only Star in My Blue Heaven," and "You Are My Sunshine"? They all became great Autry hits. I think a lot of it was because of the genuine sincerity in his voice. He would have been a country music great even if he hadn't become a cowboy star.

Not too many people remember it, but he started on radio. He may well have been the one who put WLS on the map, as a featured artist on the station's *National Barn Dance*. There were millions of people who became Gene Autry fans, long before he went to Hollywood.

The national trend on radio was for early morning and noontime country music shows and then a full-blown barn dance on Saturday night. Aside from the Opry and the *National Barn Dance*, there was the *Iowa Barn Dance* on WHO, Iowa City; the *Sunset Valley Barn Dance* on KSTP, Minneapolis–St. Paul; the *Wheeling Jamboree* on WWVA in Wheeling, West Virginia, and the *Old Dominion Barn Dance* on WRVA, Richmond. And there were barn dances on KMOX in St. Louis, WSB in Atlanta and even WMCA and WHN in New York. WHN even had a show called *The Village Barn Dance,* which originated in Greenwich Village.

Some of the greatest country music stars got their starts on small radio stations, moved on to bigger ones, and when the stations boosted their power, the local stars became national favorites. It would take a whole book to name all of them, but a few that come to mind right away are Sunshine Sue on WRVA; Cowboy Loye on WWVA; Lulu Bell and Scotty, the Hoosier Hot Shots, Bill Monroe and the Monroe Brothers, George Gobel, Homer and Jethro, and Red Foley on WLS; Bob Wills and the Texas Playboys on KVOO in Tulsa; Pappy Cheshire and the Hill-Billy Champions on KMOX; Zeke Manners and Elton Britt on WMCA: Tex Ritter on WHN: Fiddlin' John Carson and The Skillet Lickers on WSXB, and Johnny and Jack, Webb Pierce, and Faron Young on KWKH in Shreveport.

Every station had at least one big star, some had several. And while all this was going on throughout the entire country, there were stations popping up south of the border in Mexico. They were called "X" stations because their call letters began with X. The most famous was XERA in Villa Acuña, which was just across the Rio Grande from Del Rio,

Texas. A doctor named J. R. Brinkley, who was rumored to be some kind of shady character because he had lost his broadcasting license in Kansas, went to Mexico and put together the station, and while the clear-channel stations like WSM and WWVA and WLS beamed out fifty thousand watts, it was reported that XERA blasted away with half a million watts. Why, you could pick it up anywhere in the Western Hemisphere. People said you could pick it up by putting your ear against a barbed-wire fence.

It was the late-night standard for a generation of radio listeners. They sold plastic Jesuses, baby chicks, and patent medicines. One of their early stars was Cowboy Slim Rinehart, the King of the Border Stations. Slim played two or three songs and then the radio pitchman came on and started his spiel. I don't know whether Slim's playing got people in the "buying mood," or whether the pitchman was that good, but people bought those things they were selling. They bought them by the millions. It didn't matter what they were. I went into the post office one day and you couldn't hear anything but the sound of baby chicks—peeps. I thought I had gone into a poultry farm or a henhouse.

"What's with all the peeps?" I asked Josh, the fellow behind the counter.

"That damn Mexican radio station's sellin' peeps, that's what's with all the peeps," he grumbled. "Hell, I thought I was rid of all that damn chicken squawk when I ran away from the farm, but now that's all I hear. And you smell this place. I mean, just *smell*. Damn."

"Look at it this way, Josh," I said. "They could be selling pigs."

"Well, I'd quit," he said. "That's what I'd do. I'd quit. Oughta be a law against those hillbilly stations. But you know," and he calmed down, and he looked out over the counter and off into the hills, "that Slim Rinehart sure can play."

"How many chicks you buy?" I asked.

"Those three boxes over by the back door are mine," he said.

XERA attracted a lot of top talent, including the Carter Family, who left Virginia for a while to live across the river from Texas. Their records had made them famous, but it was the Mexican radio station that enabled a lot of people to hear them who might not otherwise have the chance. A lot of people couldn't afford to buy records. Their songs—"Dixie Darling," "Wildwood Flower," "Foggy Mountain," "My Clinch Mountain Home," "False-hearted Lover," "On the Rock Where Moses Stood," "Gathering Flowers From the Hillside," and "Beyond the River"—were classics, and they had a tremendous influence on many aspiring country musicians. They were "parlor" entertainers, with a simple instrumental style and voices that were a little flat but easy to listen to, and they had a rhythmic beat. It was fortunate that they were to become ambassadors of country music for so many. They did an hour show in the morning and an hour at night, so they became very popular on radio in the thirties.

Country performers popped up all over the place. Up in Akron, Ohio, a man named Louis Marshall Jones won a talent contest and, with the fifty-dollar prize, he bought himself a better guitar. He had won the contest by developing a singing, playing, and yodeling style from listening to radio. From there he went on to join the great radio program *Lum and Abner* and later wound up in West Virginia, first on WWVA and later on the Sagebrush Roundup on WMMN in Fairmont. But by then he had developed into a comic character who wore a bushy false mustache, a worn hat, baggy pants and suspenders. He had chosen the name of Grandpa Jones. Few today realize how good a banjo player he is. They think of him mostly as a comic, but as Grandpa Jones he delighted radio audiences from Kentucky to Boston. You see, radio performers moved around a lot, so people everywhere were getting to know a lot of country performers. They heard them on local stations and on the big, powerful clear-channel stations. The range of some was astounding, much more than today, because there weren't so many stations to drown them out. WSM, for example, was a network in itself, covering everything from the Rockies to Florida.

Doc Stevens owned a corner drug store in Knoxville and, as in most towns in those days, the drug store was where most people met. If they weren't inside at the soda fountain, they were standing on the corner in front. Drugs had a much different meaning in those days. But this particular drug store was also where a lot of the local musicians hung out. Musicians also had a different image in those days.

For some reason, Doc Stevens took a liking to me. He had heard me play and he knew I was trying to put together my own band, so he built an outdoor stage in the vacant lot beside the store. I talked local people into coming over to our stage to perform. It was a sort of homespun talent show, and it wasn't bad for the Coke and ice cream business either.

The stage was maybe twenty feet square and was up about four feet from the parking-lot level, resting on telephone poles that had been sunk in the ground and cut off to the proper height. A lot of show business people talk about the smell of greasepaint, but to me the smell of show business was creosote—from the old telephone poles.

It was a little on the rickety side and often the whole thing would feel like it was swaying to the beat of the band, which it probably was. Bill Norman, who was a fine little fiddle player, said one day, "Hell, Roy, one more chorus of 'Turkey in the Straw' and I swear I'd of got seasick up there." And once the stage got to rockin' so bad that Lonnie Wilson, who played guitar, fell off. One minute he was right there, strummin' away, and the next minute he was gone. Bill nudged me and said, "Where'd Lonnie go, Roy?"

"Beats me," I said, "but the melody sure got thin all of a sudden."

About that time, Lonnie pulled himself up out of the

bushes and said, "Damn, a feller could get hurt playin' hillbilly music."

Bill and Lonnie and I became good friends. And not too bad a band, either. We started playing a few square dances in the area, filling in at times with my brother Spot and a friend named Red Jones. We branched out to hoedowns, which was the country term for everybody getting together and having a good time, with hillbilly music as the central part of the get-together.

We had a lot of confidence in our group, so we entered a *real* amateur show at the Tennessee Theater, Bill and Lonnie and me. Those guys who came along thirty years later may think they invented the name "Rolling Stones," but they're wrong. We did.

The first thing we all noticed about the stage at the Tennessee Theater was how solid it was. And how dark it was out there beyond the stage. It was like playing Doc Stevens's stage at night, with no lights in the parking lot. But we gave it all we had, and what an interesting highlight it would have made to this whole story if we had won the contest. But scratch the highlight. We lost.

It wasn't that we were bad, it was just that there was so much good talent around. Everybody was playing everywhere in those days. There were different groups, but most of them were playing the same kind of music, so there was a lot of competition. Times were tough, but there were a lot of talent shows. It only cost a dime or so to get in and people could be entertained for several hours, so there was always a good house. The people who put on the shows didn't have any overhead at all, so it was almost all profit for them. They paid the winners five or ten bucks and gave some merchandise to the next two or three places. Hell, we played one talent show, finished third and each of us won a pair of socks. But it didn't matter to me at all. I wanted experience and I was getting it.

This life of playing for peanuts went on for over a year, and it looked like my career was never going one step beyond it, until one day a group that called themselves the Tennessee Crackerjacks came to Doc Stevens's stage. They sounded real good. Jess Easterday played guitar and mandolin, Clell Summey was on Dobro guitar, and Bob Wright played mandolin. They had everything it took. Everything, that is, but a leader. Well, I knew immediately where they could find one.

"Fellas," I said. "Shake hands with your new leader. I'm Roy Acuff, and I've got show business *experience*. I've been on the road."

It was the start—the real start—of my musical career. I mean, there had been other starts—the medicine show, the stage at Doc Stevens's, the talent shows, the hoedowns, and all that—but this was a real band. I knew it the minute we played our first tune together, which was "Maple on the Hill." Every so often a person gets that feeling that what he's doing is right for him. That band was right for me.

I had saved a little money from the medicine show, so I bought Doc Hauer's old REO sedan and then went to a junkyard and bought another one just like it for parts. I rebuilt the REO and we made a trailer to haul the instruments. The Tennessee Crackerjacks were ready for the assault on the world of show business. But the world of show business wasn't exactly waiting with bated breath for the Tennessee Crackerjacks. We got a few jobs here and there for a dollar or two a performance. And at times we played for nothing. Just for the exposure, we told ourselves.

We hung out a lot at WROL. The truth of the matter was that we pestered the hell out of them at WROL. I think it was just to get us off their backs, but finally they offered us a program on the air. It was sponsored by "Dr. Hamilton, Dentist."

My career, at this point, had gone from Dr. Hauer to Dr. Stevens to Dr. Hamilton. But, at last, my music was going out over the airwaves.

In true radio style, we moved on pretty quickly. Lowell Blanchard, who had the *Mid-Day Merry-Go-Round* at

WNOX, offered us a spot there, so we switched stations. It turned out to be a very good move, because within a few weeks we moved into the fifteen-hundred-seat Market Hall. We played to a full house every day, from noon until one o'clock, and we got fifty cents each. Every day. They charged a nickle admission. It was sponsored by Scalf's Indian River Tonic, which kept my medical record intact. That was one of the nation's first local, continuous-running country music programs. We stayed only eight months, but the program ran for years, giving career starts to such artists as Pee Wee King, Bill Carlisle, Archie Campbell, Johnny and Jack, and Kitty Wells. It was one of the most important radio shows in the history of country music. And it gave us a real name in show business. Real show business.

Bill Carlisle, who played rhythm guitar on the Opry for years. (WSM photo by Les Leverett)

That name was to change when we moved back to WROL to start our own noontime show. We were tuning up one day when the engineer, by mistake, switched to the studio, sending us out over the air before we were supposed to be. Allen Stout, the announcer, offered a word of explanation to the radio audience: "After all, folks," he said, "they're just a bunch of crazy Tennesseans." The name stuck.

The Crazy Tennesseans stayed at WROL for a long time. We did noon shows, opened the station in the morning and filled in at various times during the day and night. Life at a small radio station in those days was about as unglamorous as one could imagine. For one thing, we had to be there by five in the morning, awake and ready to play. Then we had to hang around the station until noon, do that show, and wait to see what afternoon spot we might have. And all this for five dollars a week. It wasn't exactly the big time. But it was experience, and we were getting a lot of mail, which was the barometer of a band's performance. People felt a sort of kinship with radio performers, and they wrote to them to tell them so or to request certain songs. Our mail got bigger and bigger, even though our paychecks didn't.

And the mail was interesting. For one thing, it amused us to read what people pictured our surroundings to be. Most of the letters referred to our "real big studio," or to us up there "with all those people and all those machines." I guess the listeners had imagined a radio broadcasting station to be a pretty elaborate layout, when, in fact, it was just the opposite.

When we did the early morning show, for example, there was only one other person there—the engineer. He sat in a tiny room, in front of a small panel with maybe five or six switches on it and a couple of dials. There was a window between his "control room" and our "studio." And it was just a plain old house window—the kind that raises and lowers. Our studio was a room about sixteen feet by twenty feet with an old mohair sofa and a couple of chairs and one microphone. There wasn't any sound-deadening material on the walls and there weren't any windows, except the one between the two rooms. There were three light fixtures that hung down from the ceiling, just like the ones in the drug store at the corner. Nothing could have been more plain.

But a lot of music went out from studios just like ours. Practically every country music performer of the period got started in surroundings just like ours, and I'm sure they got the same kind of letters from the same kind of fans who thought they were playing in some sort of mechanical jungle.

But as simple as it was, it worked. We came in, said "good morning" to Hal, the engineer, and went to work. It was the original "no-frills" side of show business. The only problems we ever had were when Hal dozed off, which he did about twice a week. The only job he had other than flipping switches was to watch the clock—which we also did. There was a sheet of paper taped to the wall where we both could see it, telling exactly when the commercials were to be played. Most of the time on the early show, the commercials were in the form of transcriptions, which were big records. There wasn't any sense to paying an announcer a salary to come in that early, so Hal would give us the signal and then work in a transcription between songs. Occasionally we got to the time for a commercial break and the only sound we heard was the sound of Hal snoring. Somebody would go over and tap on the window and he would frantically put the pick-up arm from the phonograph turntable on the transcription and the commercial would go out over the airwaves.

One morning Hal was having a particularly hard time staying awake—he must have had a bad night, or maybe it was a good one—and he went to sleep three times, and every time we woke him up, he played the same commercial. Martha White flour sure got plenty of air time, but I'll bet some of the other sponsors were awfully upset.

By the time we did the *Mid-Day Merry-Go-Round,* the whole operation had gotten pretty professional—well, as professional as it was going to get. The whole staff for the station

Playing the fiddle during the Knoxville days of my career. (WSM Archives)

had come to work and we did the show in the big auditorium, in front of an audience, so it was a far cry from the morning show. When I look back, it's the early show I think of most, although the noon show did more for all our careers. It was some show.

But things like that were happening all over at country music stations. Chet Atkins tells the story about the time at WSM radio—on the morning show, naturally—when the engineers played a joke on Tom Hansserd, one of the announcers who took his job too seriously. There wasn't much time for serious people back then. So they put a tiny speaker in one of those big, oval RCA B-44 microphones and wired it to the control booth. After setting the clock ahead five minutes, they gave Tom his cue. Speaking into a dead mike, he said, in his best voice, "Good morning, ladies and gentlemen, it's time for the six o'clock news."

The microphone spoke back to him: "Get away, you're too close. I'm tired of you spitting on me every morning. Get away."

Tom stood frozen, staring at the microphone. He thought he had gone crazy, and he was afraid to say anything about it to anyone. He just turned and walked out of the studio. They had to run after him and tell him what had happened. When he went back on for the real news, though, he stood way back from the mike.

Archie Campbell came to Knoxville, and he did a fifteen-minute segment from time to time with the Crazy Tennesseeans. He added some life to the group by portraying a character named Grandpap. He also got us free passes to the Roxy Theater, where they had a girlie show. It wasn't a stripper show or anything like that, but they had girls and we didn't turn down the passes. After all, man cannot live by fiddle alone.

Archie was a funny and talented man and we all knew that he would someday become a big star, but I thought it would be because of his voice and not his comedy routines. He had a good voice, and that was what I was convinced it took to get any group to the top. What is referred to today as a "lead singer" almost didn't exist in those days. Except with the Crazy Tennesseans, and I filled that role. I sang nearly every song, but I had to tone it down a little for radio because I had learned to sing so strong with the medicine show. I got a lot of mail.

Archie Campbell later in his career. (WSM photo by Les Leverett)

The rivalry between WROL and WNOX was a fierce but friendly one. Lowell Blanchard was constantly trying to outdo Cas Walker at WROL. Cas was a local grocer who had found out that he could sell a whole lot of groceries over the radio. The two men were so closely identified with their stations that when people burned out their radio tubes—which they did often—they would go to the store and ask for the "Cas Walker tube" or the "Lowell Blanchard tube."

Cas was a great fan of bluegrass music. He called it "jumping up and down music." He said, "If you can get a child to jump up and down, that's good, because he's happy. And if you make the child happy, you make the parents happy. And they buy groceries." The list of bluegrass musicians who worked at WROL at one time or another sounds like the Blue Book of bluegrass: Lester Flatt and Earl Scruggs, the Brewster Brothers, the Cope Brothers, the Webster Brothers, the Osborne Brothers, and the Bailey Brothers.

Obviously we couldn't live for too long on what we made by appearing on the radio, so WROL gave us the opportunity to go out at night and do road shows. Road shows were as much the mainstay of early performers as anything anybody did. All of the regular performers did them. And the stories connected with them were many.

We would determine from all the mail where we were most popular, and then we would contact somebody in that town— either the local school or a church group or any group where one of us had any contacts—and let them know that we would be available to come up there for a one-night appearance. Once we got a date set, we were allowed to announce on our radio programs that we would appear in, say, Clinton or Sevierville or Dandridge—wherever we were going. Then we would send posters to the organization that sponsored the show and hope that they got them put up. And I'll tell you, there were times when we got to a schoolhouse or wherever we were playing and found all of the posters right there in a pile.

We split the proceeds, usually seventy percent to us and thirty percent to the sponsoring group. There weren't many big towns, so we played to crowds of fifty or one hundred people, who paid twenty-five cents for adult admissions and maybe a dime for kids. You can see that we weren't getting rich on that either. Our goal became a hundred-dollar house, which seemed like a fortune to us. We needed it because the "parts" REO was about gone. Nearly the only thing left was the body, because we had scavenged every other part for the one we drove to the shows.

The daily routine became tougher. We signed on the station with the farm report, the news and then our music, stayed around for the noontime show, and usually an afternoon show, then loaded into the REO and took off for some spot back in the woods where we were going to play that night. At times it took us several hours to get there, because many of the roads weren't even paved. But we traveled those old gravel back roads and we put up with all sorts of hardships—except we didn't look on them as hardships. It was what you had to do. There were trees over the road, and creeks up and, in the winter, icy roads, which was the worst, because we had never heard of winter tires. But we never missed a show. Oh, we were there right at showtime a few times, but we made it. At times we got out of the car and went right on stage, with no time to change and little time to tune up.

And if we did have time to change, it usually was a pretty primitive arrangement. We played schoolhouses mostly, but there were courthouse appearances and church basements, and any sort of place where there was a stage. And most times it was a makeshift affair. When we played courthouses we usually appeared right in the courtroom, and the bench where the judge sat was our stage.

There seldom was an actual room that we could use to change into our stage costumes. We changed in the car and in alleys, and we put our street clothes in the instrument cases. We played some ragged places. You usually couldn't see to get around backstage—if there even was a backstage—and there was always somebody falling over something.

We played in places that didn't even have electricity, old schoolhouses that were lighted by kerosene. To this day I get a nostalgic twinge when I smell kerosene, because I can't begin to count the number of places we played that were lighted by lanterns.

We ran out of gas and blew tires and had to walk for miles at times for help. And when we got to the place where we were to appear, one of us sold tickets and another took them up. It wasn't that we didn't trust the people there, it's just that, well, money is hard for some people to handle, and it was especially hard in those days when there was so little of it.

We usually made five or six dollars a night each, and we got back at times so late that there wasn't any point in going to bed, so we would just go to the station and either sleep in the car or just sit on the steps until it was time to sign on the air. Many times, Cas Walker arrived to find us sitting on the steps, asleep.

Grandpa Jones tells the story of when he was working at WMMN in Fairmont, West Virginia, when he was doing the same thing up there—going out for road shows at night in towns like Belington and Jane Lew and everywhere, and he was so poor that he couldn't afford to buy a new alarm clock. He really needed one, because he was only getting a few hours sleep each night, and he couldn't wake up on his own. So he would take the old clock that he had and make do. It was one of the old kind that had two bells on top and an arm that vibrated between them, making the alarm sound. Well, the bells had broken off, so he would set it for about five-thirty, because he, too, was doing the early show, and he'd place the clock right on the edge of the nightstand in his little room in the boardinghouse. When the clock went off, the arm would vibrate the clock right off the stand, and when the clock hit the floor, it woke him up. It lasted a couple of years.

But we all played for anybody who wanted us. One night we played for an audience up in Sneadville, Tennessee, right near the Virginia border. To give you some idea of how far back in the woods it was, they had just gotten their first telephone in the town the week we appeared there. Not the first *dial* phone. The first *telephone*, period. Archie Campbell went with us, and as was the case with most of our shows, we opened with a couple of numbers, did a comedy skit, then a hymn or two and some more comedy and more tunes, and so on. There was always a lot of comedy in our show, but it was good, clean humor. I mean, I have always put on a "family" show, and I think it's one of the reasons we drew so well. People brought their kids and aunts and uncles and grand-mothers, and we always played to a full house, as small as the room might have been.

Well, this one night, the audience was made up mostly of what they called "Mulungens," which was a sort of mixed breed of people. I don't know exactly what the mixture was, but they were kind and wonderful people. Archie did his Grandpap routine, and I mean he hit them with every joke and every funny routine he had. He didn't get a single laugh. Not even a snicker. And he was using material that had them in the aisles in most places.

After the show, when we were changing into our street clothes, Archie came to me with this long face and said, "Roy, I don't understand it. I mean, I let 'em have everything I got, and they didn't laugh once. Hell, I thought I was going to make them *cry* instead of laugh. You reckon I'm on some kind of blacklist up here, Roy?"

I assured him that he wasn't and that everybody has a night when the material doesn't work, but he was still de-jected as all get out when we left the place. Outside we found out why they hadn't laughed. They were lined up to shake hands with us—primarily with Archie. One of them said to Archie, "You know, when you told that joke about the billy-goat, why, I thought I'd laugh out loud."

It turned out it was their belief that we were their guests in that town, and that they were to treat us with respect. They were to pay attention and be polite, and to laugh out loud would have been considered rude.

Our crowds became consistently larger. I still hear artists talking about the good old days when they played to three or four people. We never did that. We always played to full houses.

One reason was that we always got there. As I saved a little money, I put it back into my shows. Whenever possible, I would either go to the town a few days early, and put up the posters myself and maybe even take out a little ad in the local newspaper, or see to it that somebody I knew did it for me. I didn't leave anything to chance.

Just as soon as I could afford it, I bought a new car. I sort of hated to see the old REO go, because it represented my start in show business, but I had to have something that was more dependable. We were getting requests to go farther and farther away from Knoxville, because our popularity had spread. We were playing bigger and bigger houses, and the days of the old "kerosene circuit" appeared to be behind us. We were playing to hundred-dollar houses night after night. And then some.

5

. . . I'll be joyfully carried to meet Him, on the wings of that Great Speckled Bird.

There was a fellow named Charlie Swain working for WROL in 1935 who had a group called the Black Shirts. I was listening to them one day after we had done one of our programs when he sang a chorus of a song I had heard years before. It was called "The Great Speckled Bird" and I had been trying to get the words to it ever since I had started playing. The words were sung to the melody of "I'm Thinking Tonight of My Blue Eyes," and it impressed me so much as being a sincere, religious song. It was beautiful:

> *When He cometh, descending from heaven*
> *On the clouds as He writes in His word*
> *I'll be joyfully carried to meet Him*
> *On the wings of the Great Speckled Bird.*

I later learned that the Reverend Guy Smith had written five or six verses to the song. They were based on the ninth verse of the twelfth chapter of Jeremiah in the Bible: "My heritage is unto me as a speckled bird, the birds round about are against her." So I asked Charlie if he would write down the words for me and he did. I paid him fifty cents for the words but I didn't use them until after Charlie left town, because I figured that it was his song while he was there. As much as I wanted to add the song to my show, I was honor bound not to.

The first time I sang it on the air, I got more favorable mail about it and more requests to sing it again than for any song I had ever done. My original feeling for it was right, and I suppose this came through when I sang it. I've noticed over the years that the songs I have a real love or a strong feeling for are the ones that come across best. I've never been able to do much with a song I didn't like.

The long wait to get the words to the song and then to sing it on the air and in personal appearances paid off. In 1936 a man named William R. Callaway, who was the A&R man (artists and repertoire) for the American Record Company, visited Knoxville, looking for talent. We didn't know he was in the audience for our noon show at WROL, but afterwards he came backstage and said, "Roy, I enjoyed your singing and I like the band, but most of all I like the way you did 'The Great Speckled Bird.' I've been looking for someone who could do that song for about a year now. Would you be interested in recording it for the American Record Company?"

Was I interested? We signed a contract that day to go to Chicago for a recording session, but I wasn't as excited as I should have been, maybe because I always felt that he wanted "The Bird" instead of me.

We went to Chicago in October of 1936. I had Clell Summey on Dobro guitar, Red Jones on bass, Dynamite Hatcher on harmonica and Jess Easterday on guitar. We stayed at the Knickerbocker Hotel and the session lasted for several days because we recorded twenty songs. Twenty!

Before that recording session, I experimented with many instrumental combinations but settled on what I had always used. I always felt that it was best to leave most of the instrumentation to the other members of the band, and most of the singing to me. We never used much of the Western-swing flourishes, but stuck to the style of the old mountain string band, with a fiddle, rhythm guitar, string bass, five-string banjo (played with the old-time frailing technique), and Dobro guitar. Once in a while we used a harmonica or mandolin or even a piano, but the instrument I always favored was the Dobro. I still do. In fact, to this day, I've never really changed the structure of the band.

I never tried to have any of my boys sing close harmony with me because I always wanted my band to sound like the music of the mountain churches—what I had heard when I was a boy. And I never sang any cowboy or Western songs. There were enough fellows around who were good at that, so I just left it to them. My songs were always more along sacred lines. I guess I was giving the people a choice. Many of the other singers had gone to Western songs and Western clothes—it was a new style—but I wanted to stick to the more *traditional* country music approach.

With another recording contract, I felt comfortable and successful enough to ask Mildred Douglas to marry me. I had been dating her for a long time and with the sixteen dollars a week she was making at Lane Drug Store, I figured we could make it. We got married on Christmas Day 1936. It proved to be the best thing that ever happened to me.

I tried time and again to get on the Grand Ole Opry but by 1937 I had just about given up. I felt that I had gone as far as I would ever go in Knoxville, so I decided that it was time to move on. I got out a road map and just picked a spot. Indianapolis looked like a good central location, about half-way between Nashville, with the Opry, and Chicago, with the *National Barn Dance*. From there, I reasoned, I could go either way. And either way would beat where I was.

Pee Wee King had come to Knoxville to play on radio and a few months earlier I had gone to Nashville to talk to Joe L. Frank, an agent, about Pee Wee and me coming to the Opry. There had been no response. But this time I called Joe and asked if he could get me on station WIRE in Indianapolis.

The Life and Good Times of Country Music

"It'd be a good spot for me, J. L., because, you see, I could go . . ."

I didn't even finish the sentence. Joe said, "Roy, you still interested in a guest spot on the Opry?" When I told him I was, he turned to David Stone, head of WSM's Artists' Service Bureau, and asked about the prospects. "How 'bout Saturday night, Roy?"

We were on our way.

It turned out that Kirk and Sam McGee were playing up in West Virginia and David Stone was looking for a replacement

This is the band that I brought to the Opry in 1938. From left to right: Clell Summey, Jess Easterday, Imogene (Tiny) Sarrett, myself, and Red Jones. They all left to return to Knoxville in 1939, and a new band was formed. (From the collection of Les Leverett)

for them when I called. In fact, Kirk and Sam had teamed up with Arthur Smith to form the Dixieliners, and they had become the first act ever booked out of WSM. So we became the first replacement act.

David Stone asked me to come over with the boys—Jess, Clell and Red—but he really wanted me to play the fiddle. He didn't say a word about my singing, but I felt that I would do much better if I sang. After all, that's what had worked so well for me in Knoxville, and I thought this was my greatest chance for success. It's not that I thought my voice was that much better than anybody else's, it's just that it was that much *different*. And there were no bands with a lead singer on the Opry then.

I hadn't patterned my voice after anybody. Most singers at that time tried to sound like Rudy Vallee or Bing Crosby or Russ Colombo. And if that didn't work, then they tried to yodel like Jimmie Rodgers. I didn't try any of those things, I just tried to sing out, and with as much feeling as I could get.

Some of the regulars on the Opry in those days were Uncle Dave Macon, the Fruit Jar Drinkers, the Possum Hunters, the Gulley Jumpers, Herman Crook and the Crook Brothers, Curly Fox, Jack Shook, the Missouri Mountaineer, the Delmore Brothers, the Dixieliners and Sarie and Sally—all experienced acts. To say I was nervous when I walked on the stage at the Dixie Tabernacle on Fatherland Street in Nashville in October 1937 would be the understatement of my entire life. But I also was *determined*.

I remembered the story Cas Walker had told me about the first time Pappy Beaver ever appeared on WROL. He was so nervous that he said, "I want to dedicate this song to my father and daddy." "I hope they both hear it," Cas said.

I opened with "Old Hen Cackle," a traditional fiddle song. I was so nervous that I played back of the bridge about as much as I played in front of it. But I got nice applause and that calmed me down some. I looked at the boys and nodded. They

This is the way I looked at the time of my first Grand Ole Opry appearance. (WSM Archives)

George Wilkerson (second from left) and his Fruit Jar Drinkers, one of the earliest groups to perform on the Grand Ole Opry. (WSM Archives)

knew what I meant. We went right into "The Great Speckled Bird."

I crooned it as much as I could, feeling that if I gave them the old medicine show voice it would probably knock the station right off the air. The more I crooned, the more I realized it was a mistake. The powerful equipment of WSM could have handled anything I had to give, but I didn't know that. The only thing I knew was that my voice sounded to me like a whining pup's.

Everyone was polite to me. The audience applauded politely, J. L. Frank congratulated me politely. David Stone said goodbye politely. And somehow I felt that the "goodbye" was a final one for me at the Grand Ole Opry. Politely.

The trip back to Knoxville was a whole lot longer than the one to Nashville. The boys tried to cheer me up, but it didn't work. I hardly said a word during the long trip on those old two-lane highways. And when I went to work the next morning, the old spark wasn't there. Cas sensed the problem; I guess he had talked with the boys. He said, "Listen, Roy, I heard the show and I thought it was really swell. I mean, you knocked 'em dead." Polite again.

"Thanks, Cas," I said. "I'll be all right."

But I wasn't. I even gave up the idea of moving to Indianapolis, because I figured Knoxville was about all that I could ever handle.

As usual, Mildred was a great comfort to me when I was so down. She always knew what to say to cheer me up, and within a few days she had me right back to my old self. It wasn't so much that I had resigned myself to WROL in Knoxville as that she actually had me convinced that I would be better off as the "big duck in the little puddle." "After all, Roy," she said, "you're a big star here. Over there in Nashville you'd be just one of the group. I mean, just look at all those artists who have been there for years. There's not one of them as popular in Knoxville as you are." Mildred should have been a psychiatrist.

In fact, I had forgotten completely about the Opry. Well, at least, I didn't talk about it anymore. To tell you the truth, I've always *told* people that I completely forgot about it, but I never did. I thought about it every waking moment. But in February of 1938, I got a letter from David Stone, offering me another chance. An audition was scheduled for February 5.

It was cold and rainy on that Saturday night at the Opry and Joe Frank tried to calm me down backstage while David introduced me. "Was Mickey Mouse a dog or a cat, Roy?" he asked. "How the hell do I know, Joe? Don't ask me stupid questions like that before I go on the air," I snapped. But it worked, I was still trying to figure out that stupid question as I approached the mike.

Clell played the opening of "The Bird" on the Dobro (I think it was the first time the Dobro guitar was ever used on the Opry), and when I sang this time I put the full force and the full feeling into it. I sang one verse and then, you know, I almost went into shock. My knees started to shake and I thought I was going to throw up. Clell saw me sort of sag and

Clell Summey, dressed in his comic Cousin Jody outfit. He was one mean Dobro guitar player. (WSM Archives)

he laid down another chorus and verse of the best Dobro guitar I think I had ever heard. It pepped me up, and I sang the second verse. And the third and fourth.

The audience reaction was much better, but somehow I felt I still hadn't sold the Opry executives. Had I failed again? I wondered as we made the tortuous drive back to Knoxville. As the rain beat down on the windshield of the Pontiac and mile after mile of lonely, winding mountain road unfolded in front of us, I was living the true-life "Ballad of Roy Acuff," as sad a story as I could imagine.

Once again it was depression-time in the Smoky Mountains. But something entirely different was happening in Nashville. By the middle of the next week, sack after sack of mail was rolling into WSM. It was the first time the station had ever gotten a response like that to any Opry act. The listeners of the Opry had gotten the soul message that I had tried to put across. "The Great Speckled Bird" and Roy Acuff had gotten through.

I got a telegram from David, offering me a tentative assignment on the Opry. It didn't offer anything permanent, but it was the sweetest telegram I ever received. The next day, they forwarded the mail to me, and it all said basically the same thing: "We want Roy Acuff and his 'Great Speckled Bird.' "

Then on February 10, 1938, I got a letter from David. I remember the date because I still have the letter. It read:

Dear Roy:

I am in receipt of your telegram advising that you will be here for the programs starting the 19th. I will book you for a spot on the Grand Ole Opry and also a series of 7:00 AM programs starting Monday, February 21st.

Since writing to you we have arranged for a commercial spot on the Grand Ole Opry for which there will be a small salary as long as the commercial runs. Of course, we reserve the right to change the Opry schedule, but as long as you are on a commercial spot there will be something for you.

I am teaming you up with the Delmore Brothers for several personal appearances. These boys have tremendous popularity in this territory, but they cannot build or manage their own unit so I think it would be a great combination for the two acts. I think I can get some good dates right away and start you out as soon as you get here. This will save a great deal of time in getting your build-up with the WSM audience.

We will talk it over in detail when you get here and I

feel sure that we can make satisfactory arrangements. If you have any photographs, cuts, or mats, please mail them to me at once so that we can get publicity started.

Very truly yours,
David

We made our first appearance on the Opry as regulars on February 19, 1938, and the very next day we made our first personal appearance as a WSM *act*. We went to Dawson Springs, Kentucky.

Now that we were Grand Ole Opry "stars," I expected the whole world to change. It did. Instead of playing a one-room schoolhouse, we played a *two*-room schoolhouse. Somehow I had expected the change to be a little more earth-shattering.

To make matters worse, it had started to snow pretty hard by the time we got to the schoolhouse. It was our first night as Opry road show performers and I was sure we were going to play to the janitor and the little old lady who lived across the road.

"Tell me the part again about life in the big time, Roy," Clell said as he slipped on the icy rocks leading to the school. He was loaded to the chin with guitar cases and sound equipment. I had just as big a load. Jess was already inside with Imogene Sarrett, who we had added to our group. Everybody called her "Tiny." Red was back at the car getting the rest of the gear.

"Shush," I said, "you want Red and Jess and Tiny to get discouraged?"

"Well, if they ain't discouraged already, they just ain't payin' attention," he said. "I mean, I don't know if you've noticed or not, but our car's the only one here."

I had noticed.

But by the time we got set up, a few people had come in. And by the time we were ready, the place was filled. I mean, every seat was occupied and there wasn't any more room to stand in the back. And they cheered and stomped their feet after every song we did. And they roared at our comedy routines.

I don't know if it proved that we really were that good or if the people were just starved for entertaiment, but after the show, I said to the man who helped us sell and take up tickets, "I was afraid there for a minute that we might not have anybody here tonight; I mean, when we first got here, you know? Why you 'spose they came out on such a miserable night?"

"Well, Mister Acuff," he said, "y'all come from the Opry. Why wouldn't they come out?"

It meant more to me than the sixty-two dollars we made that night.

The next morning I did my first fifteen minute segment on the early morning show at WSM. And I knew it was going all the way out to the Clinch Mountains. And maybe beyond.

Performing on the Opry with one of my early bands, as George D. Hay, the Solemn Old Judge, blows his horn. That's me with the fiddle. (From the collection of Les Leverett)

6

"For the past hour we have been listening to . . . Grand Opera, but from now on we will present 'The Grand Ole Opry.'"

—*George D. Hay*

The Grand Ole Opry definitely is a show business phenomenon. It really is. You see, this live country music radio program has been running continuously for more than fifty-seven years and it's more popular today than ever. Its history is rich and colorful. It's, well, it's just unique.

The Opry got started on November 28, 1925, on the fifth-floor studio of WSM by the National Life and Accident Insurance Company. The first performer was Uncle Jimmy Thompson, who was an eighty-year-old fiddler with a long, white beard, who said he could "fiddle the 'taters right off the vine." He also claimed that he knew more than a thousand fiddle rounds, but in the hour he was allotted he didn't get time to prove his claim.

"Fiddlesticks!" Uncle Jimmy said after the show. "A man can't git warmed up in an hour."

The announcer was George D. Hay, a real pioneer in country music show business who called himself "the Solemn Old Judge," even though he was only thirty years old. But he went back almost as far as radio itself, having been on

WMC in Memphis and WLS in Chicago before coming to Nashville. When the Judge launched that first program (actually it was called the *WSM Barn Dance*), he started a tradition that would launch country music right into the mainstream of American music and show business, a position that it might otherwise never have attained.

George D. Hay (left) introduces Uncle Jimmy Thompson on the first program of the Grand Ole Opry in 1925. (WSM Archives)

Two years later, the Solemn Old Judge gave the program its permanent name. WSM was a member of the National Broadcasting Company and also was carrying *The Music Appreciation Hour,* which was hosted by Dr. Walter Damrosch. The *WSM Barn Dance* followed that network segment with three hours of good old country music. The Judge later told me how he happened to call it the Opry.

"Dr. Damrosch," he said, "always signed off his concert a minute or so before we hit the air with our mountain minstrels and vocal trapeze performers. We must confess that the change in pace was immense. But that is part of America— fine lace and homespun cloth.

"The monitor in our Studio B was turned on, so that we would have a rough idea of the time, which was fast approaching. At about five minutes before eight, I called for silence in the studio. Out of the loudspeakers came the correct, but accented voice of Dr. Damrosch, and his words were something like this: 'While most artists realize there is no place in the classics for realism, nevertheless I am going to break one of my rules and present a composition by a young composer from Iowa, who sent us his latest number, which depicts the onrush of a locomotive . . .'

"After the announcement, the good doctor directed the symphony orchestra through the number which carried many 'shooshes' depicting an engine trying to come to a full stop. Then he closed his program with his usual sign-off.

"Our control operator gave us the signal which indicated that we were on the air . . . and I said that Dr. Damrosch told us that it is generally agreed that there is no place in the classics for realism. However, from there on out for the next three hours we will present nothing but realism . . . it will be down to earth for the earthy.

"In respectful contrast to Dr. Damrosch's presentation of the number which depicts the onrush of locomotives, we will call on one of our performers—Deford Bailey, with harmonica—to give us the country version of his 'Pan American Blues.' "

At that point, Deford Bailey, a wizard with the harmonica, played the number. At the close of it, the Judge said, "For the past hour we have been listening to music taken largely from the Grand Opera, but from now on we will present 'The Grand Ole Opry.' "

It didn't take long for the crowds to begin appearing. There were so many, in fact, that they had to create a bigger studio. They constructed Studio C, which not only had better acoustics, but also could seat five hundred people. It didn't take any time for them to outgrow Studio C, so they rented the Hillsboro Theater, which was a former movie house in Southwest Nashville.

The next move came almost as quickly, and for the same reason. They needed more space. So they moved to a huge old place across the Cumberland River on Fatherland Street called the Dixie Tabernacle. The floors were covered with sawdust and the benches were splintery and crude, so it was immediately referred to as the "Sawdust Trail."

This is where they were when I joined the Opry, but they only stayed there until July of 1938, when the Opry was moved to the new War Memorial Auditorium. At this point, they started to charge an admission to get in. Before that the Opry had been pretty much used as an insurance-buying incentive. National Life and Accident Insurance salesmen were given tickets to pass out to their prospective clients throughout the entire area, but there were still so many people who just "showed up" that they couldn't control the crowds. So they figured that if they charged a twenty-five-cent admission fee, it would curb the crowd. They were wrong, because the two-thousand-seat auditorium became too small, and they made the move into what was to become the most famous—if not the finest—auditorium the Opry was to have for many years, the old Ryman Auditorium.

The Ryman had been built in 1891 by a riverboat captain named Tom Ryman, who once had gone to a tent show to heckle the preacher. Well, Ryman not only didn't heckle the preacher, he got converted to Christianity and wound up building a church for the Reverend Sam Jones, who must

Deford Bailey in the 1930s. Deford was the first black performer to play on the Opry and one of its most popular musicians for many decades. (WSM photo by Les Leverett)

*Ryman Auditorium, home of the Grand Ole Opry from 1941 to 1974.
(Nashville Area Chamber of Commerce)*

have been a very persuasive evangelist. A balcony was added for the Confederate Veterans Reunion of 1897, which brought the capacity to well over three thousand.

The first real country band to appear on WSM was the Possum Hunters, headed by Dr. Humphrey Bate. He was a graduate of the Vanderbilt Medical School, but he loved playing the harmonica more than anything else. His daughter, Alcyone, played the piano. She was thirteen years old when she started, but she stayed on to perform for fifty years on the Opry.

There were many good traditional mountain music performers in the early days of the Opry, but it was the Solemn Old Judge who actually kept the show moving. He was a very popular announcer, who in 1924 had received 150,000 votes to become the favorite radio announcer in the country in the very first nationwide radio popularity poll of any kind. He had learned to love country music as a result of covering a news story for WMC radio, which was owned by the Memphis *Commercial Appeal.* He had befriended a large rural family in the Ozarks in searching for the story, and they took him to his first barn dance. That was his first love from that point on. "I never saw anybody have more fun than those people did that night," he said.

He always used a steamboat whistle on the Opry. He had acquired it when he was with WMC and he called it "Huspa-kena" after a little town somewhere in northern Mississippi. The whistle bacame a broadcasting ritual and a part of Saturday night Americana.

The Judge also made the phrase "It's time for the pawpaws to paw, the tall pines to pine and the old cow to slip silently away" an important part of Saturday night, because that's the way he closed the show each week.

And he gave all new performers to the Opry—including me—the same solid advice: "Keep it close to the ground."

But if the Solemn Old Judge was the solidifying factor of the Opry, Uncle Dave Macon was its first star. Uncle Dave, the "Dixie Dewdrop," joined the Opry in 1926 after several years in vaudeville.

Actually Uncle Dave had started out in the "freight" business. Except, in this case, the freight was hauled by a mule and cart, because he never did learn to drive a car or truck. The "Macon Midway Mule and Wagon Transportation Company" painted on the side of his wagon was a familiar sight

Uncle Dave Macon, the "Dixie Dewdrop" (seated), and his son Dorris could captivate an audience for hours. Uncle Dave's foot-stompin', banjo-twirlin' style became an Opry legend. (WSM Archives)

throughout the South for twenty years. And if it hadn't been for a circus that came to Nashville, he might not have gotten bitten by the show business bug. He was just a kid then and his father owned the Broadway Hotel, where the circus performers stayed. They gave little David tickets and he was hooked on show business from that point on.

But he didn't become a professional entertainer until he was forty-eight years old. He had gone to Oklahoma for a visit with relatives and he took along his banjo, as he always had on the mule-and-cart trips. He was asked to play at the neighborhood school for a drive to raise some funds for furniture for the local minister's home. His appearance was such a roaring success that he returned to Tennessee and signed with the RKO Theater circuit, where he toured all over the South, playing at RKO theaters. This led to a recording contract and finally to the Opry.

Uncle Dave had a saying that he lived by: "If life gives you a lemon, make it into lemonade."

It was just such spirit as that of the Solemn Old Judge and Uncle Dave that filled the entire Opry cast of regulars. I couldn't believe it when I first came there. Everybody was so carefree and relaxed and the backstage area—the *whole* stage, for that matter—was absolute bedlam. Everybody was running around and talking and not paying any attention to anything. I didn't see how any of the acts ever got on stage. But they had a bulletin board backstage and everybody checked it, found out what portion of the show they were on, and then went around and visited with everybody else. Miraculously, when it came time, they went on. And the group that came off took right up with the visiting and laughing.

Everybody—from Deford Bailey to the Delmore Brothers—was like one big, happy family. So much so that, even in those days in the Deep South, it didn't seem to matter much to anybody around the Opry that Deford was black. He was just a fine musician and a wonderful little man; beyond that it didn't matter what color he was.

The Life and Good Times of Country Music

It was a different situation when we went on the road; there were problems about where he could stay and even where he could eat, but it didn't bother him. I would give anything if things could have been the way they are today. But Deford had been working with Uncle Dave from the first days of the Opry, and they became good friends. There were times when Uncle Dave had to tell hotel and tourist home owners that Deford was his valet, so that he could stay in the same place. We all hated it, but we did what *we* could to make him equal. And, thank God, when he went on the stage, he *was* equal. Why, when I first came to town, Deford was one of the real stars.

One night in Jackson, Mississippi, Uncle Dave and Deford had been turned away by about half a dozen tourist homes. It was getting late and they were tired, so at what they figured was about the last stop, Uncle Dave told the sleepy-eyed man at the door of the tourist home, "You got two rooms, Cap? For me and my brother out there?"

"Sure do," he said.

"Okay, Deford, come on in," he hollered into the darkness.

Well, when Deford came into the light, the man's mouth dropped open. "Is, uh, is . . . er, that your *brother*?" he stammered.

With that, Deford took the man by the arm and sort of led him off to the side and said to him, like it was in confidence, "Don't tell him, mister, but he had a colored Daddy. Might hurt his feelin's."

The man's mouth was still hanging open as the two of them went inside to their rooms.

Right from the beginning—clear back to the medicine show days, you might say—I've always tried to keep things as lively and entertaining as possible on the stage. I hated to see a dead stage, so I tried to entertain the folks as much as possible all the time I was up there. Most of the time, I played it by ear. I tried to listen to what the act in front of me was doing, and then I tried to figure out what the one following me might do; then I tried to do something different. I knew my opening number and that's about all.

I added the yo-yo to my act to entertain the folks while the radio was playing commercials. And then I put the fiddle-balancing act in the "dead time" portion of the show. While the commercial was going out over the air, I was up there on the stage, balancing the fiddle and the bow on my chin. The folks listening on the radio at home thought the audience was applauding for the commercial. The sponsors loved it, and it didn't matter if it was for Goo Goo candy bars or Martha White Flour, or whatever, I got letters from the sponsors saying that they wanted me to keep it up. It was fine with me, because I ate Goo Goos all the time anyway, and I was glad to give them a helping hand. Or chin.

I figured I needed to keep everybody's attention, so I was always doing something, even if it was just moving around and talking to other performers. The audience watched everything I did, so I kept their attention. My purpose was to entertain. It's why I sang so much, and it's why I featured the Dobro guitar. For one thing, my singing was different. For another, I was the only singer that didn't either yodel or sing in soft harmony. I guess it's why I became the first singing star of the Opry. I just stood out there and belted out the songs, but I belted them out with feeling.

I figured anybody could yodel. It's difficult to yodel well, but anybody can yodel halfway decent if they can sing at all; it's just a simple break in the voice. Besides, I thought that if you couldn't yodel in the blues style like Jimmie Rodgers, there wasn't any use to try it. But that didn't stop two dozen others from *trying* to imitate Jimmie. None succeeded, though.

I figured right off that I certainly wasn't going to push – Uncle Dave or Sam and Kirk McGee or people like that off the Opry, so I had to find a place where there wasn't already a star there. Singing in front of a band was it. I mean, today you

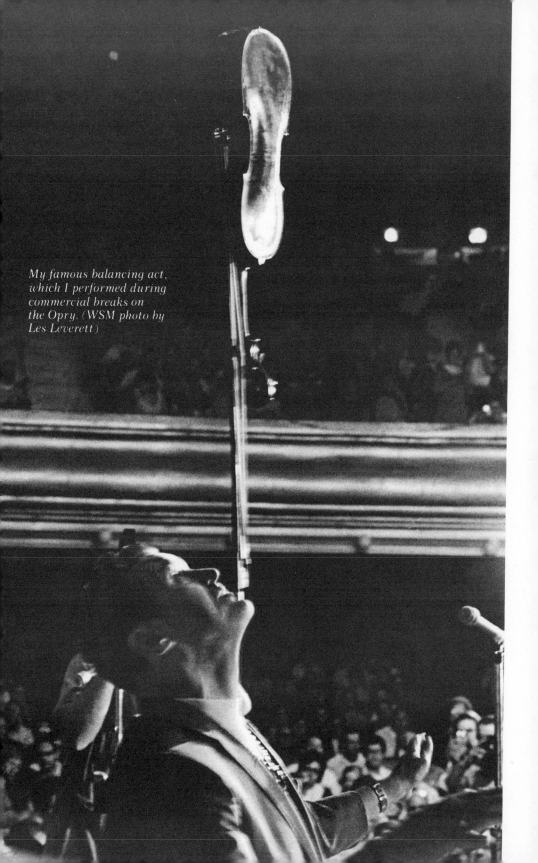

*My famous balancing act,
which I performed during
commercial breaks on
the Opry. (WSM photo by
Les Leverett)*

can get on the Opry simply by having a good record. But not then.

As for the Dobro guitar, well it, too, was different. The Dobro is sort of a cross between the original Hawaiian guitar and the more advanced electric. It uses a metal vibrating disc that amplifies it without the use of electricity. The original Hawaiian guitar—or the steel guitar, as we called it—was just too harsh for me. And the fact that most played it flat in their laps didn't set too well with me, either. I guess I've just always been for traditional music. I mean, a guitar is something that you pick up and hold against the body and caress, like a baby.

I've never been a great believer in electric. In fact, I've always been glad that the bluegrass boys have taken their stand against electric. I think it's one of the things that has made bluegrass distinctive. I don't mind electric guitars if they're turned down, but a lot of them try to knock the other performers off the stage with it. Sam McGee brought an electric guitar to the Opry in 1938, but it didn't set too well. The Judge said, "Sam, I don't think you ought to use it anymore. It's not only disturbin' to the ear but to the microphone, as well."

And the groups never used drums either. Most said they didn't need a beat, but nevertheless they were pounding their feet a lot, and some of those old hollow stages sounded a lot like drums.

With our apparent success, I decided that the name "The Crazy Tennesseeans" was a little too frivolous for the image I wanted. Besides that, it was little disrespectful to my native state, so I changed the name of the band to the Smoky Mountain Boys. But it turned out that the Smoky Mountain Boys, plus Tiny, wanted to return to the Smoky Mountains. We had some slight disagreements about the style of the music I wanted to play, and they felt they would rather be back in Knoxville anyway, so I was faced with the task of rebuilding the band. I turned to home and found my old pals

Jake Tindell from the medicine show days and Lonnie Wilson from my Stevens Drug Store stage days. Lonnie was working at a shoe store so he jumped at the chance to play again. I needed a Dobro player, so I found Pete Kirby, working at a bakery in Knoxville, and I asked him to join the group. I had used Pete from time to time to fill in for Clell and I knew he was good.

It was important to me to stay on the Opry and with the new band it looked like I could do it. I mean, once you got on you stayed. It was that simple. And you played every Saturday night, no matter where you went during the week; you got back to Nashville on Saturday night, and only a death in the family—say, your own—would excuse an absence.

One week we passed through Nashville three times. Passed through, but didn't stop. We played a church basement in Bowling Green, Kentucky, on Sunday, drove back through Nashville to get to Lynchburg, Tennessee, on Monday, went on to Birmingham and then back through town on our way to Jackson, Tennessee, on Wednesday. We turned right around and went to Chattanooga, going through Nashville again. From there we went to Atlanta. In those days, Atlanta was a hard drive from Nashville, so we got started back early Saturday morning, even though we had played a hoedown that lasted until two in the morning. And would you believe, we got forty miles from Nashville and the car broke down.

We had gone through Nashville so much that week I felt like a Trailways bus driver, and it looked like we weren't going to make the Opry on Saturday night. But we finally got the car fixed and went roaring into Nashville. Just as we got backstage, I heard the announcement: "And now, ladies and gentlemen, the Grand Ole Opry is proud to present one of your favorite acts. They've had a nice leisurely drive up from Atlanta so they're fresh as daisies for you. Here they are now, Roy Acuff and the Smoky Mountain Boys."

We looked like something the cat had drug in when we went on stage. We were greasy from working on the car, and hot and sweaty to boot. We hadn't even unpacked our instruments, let alone tuned them up, but I guess we looked so bad that the audience thought the "fresh as a daisy" part was a gag. They actually thought we had greasepaint on and had put on the grubbiest clothes we had, just for the act. I played off of it.

"We was gonna call ourselves the 'Aristocrats,' " I said, "but we figured that wasn't distinguished enough for our act."

They loved it.

7

Road show life was tough, but all of the top performers did them, and I sure wasn't going to break the tradition.

Everything hit at once for me—the Opry, the morning show on WSM and road show appearances with the Delmore Brothers. It seemed to be more than a fellow could hope for. The road show portion was designed to give me the quickest exposure because the Delmore Brothers were well known and I wasn't. But what it almost gave me was an ulcer. The first job I worked with them started out fine. I was to do a couple of numbers with my boys to warm up the crowd, but about the time I was to go on, I heard this ruckus backstage. I mean, it sounded like murder. Everybody heard it. I told the boys to go on without me while I checked what was happening backstage.

By the time I got backstage, Raybon yelled, "Alton you've whipped me for the last time. If you ever jump on me again I'll cut your guts out." Then there was a crash. Well, I wondered what I had gotten into. I really thought one of them was about to get killed, so I hurried back to the stage and introduced them.

"Ladies and gentlemen," I said, "it gives me great pleasure to introduce one of the great acts of country music, the beloved Delmore Brothers." And then I held my breath, figuring that if even *one* of them came out, I would be lucky. But the applause broke out and I turned around to see them both coming out as if nothing had happened. Something like this happened almost every night. They would get drunk and fight and then come out and play like mad. I could see why David Stone had wanted me to team up with them. I felt like a *referee*.

Dave Ackman, nicknamed "Stringbean." His funny routines made him an Opry and country music favorite for years. (WSM photo by Les Leverett)

But one Sunday afternoon in Madison, Tennessee, I reached my limit. Madison was a long drive in those days and I wasn't too happy about doing a show in the afternoon and that night to begin with, so I gave them this fine introduction and stood back and waited for someone to come out. And waited. I began to get upset. Finally I said, "Like I said, ladies and gentlemen, we're fortunate to have these brothers here today, so let's give them a big welcome," the crowd applauded for about the third time and Raybon came out *alone*. I passed him on the stage as he came out and I said to him out of the corner of my mouth, "Where the hell's Alton?" and he said, "Hell, he's layin' back there on the floor *drunk*." So Raybon went on and did the show.

After the show I called David and said, "Listen, I can't start a career like this. I mean, they're ruinin' me." So David came out and got Alton sobered up and on stage for that night's performance.

It was a bad experience, but they were really good boys, and great entertainers. It's just that they drank too much and fought too much. But back then a lot of the boys drank. They seemed to feel that they needed it to face the crowd. But a lot of them could handle it, like George Wilkerson, the leader of the Fruit Jar Drinkers; his eyes were always a little red, but you could never tell it on the stage. He went right out there and put on a good show just the same. Some people can drink and some can't. I tried it a lot in my younger days, but I soon found out that it took away too much of my thinking, so I never drank before I went on stage. I was just too interested in putting on a good show to let anything stand in the way of it.

We played a one-room schoolhouse one night on a mountaintop in West Virginia and it was so cold that we about froze to death just getting up there. You see, cars didn't have the best heaters in those days. A lot didn't have any. In fact, you always figured on being too cold in the winter and too hot in the summer. But this night it was really cold and the snow was blowing and the roads were bad.

You had to drive real slow on icy roads because the tires didn't have much traction on dry pavement, let alone icy pavement, and those West Virginia roads were bad any time of year, not to mention winter, so we were running late anyway. Well, there had been a lot of people waiting outside the schoolhouse, and the principal had let them go inside to stay warm while they waited for us. When we got there and got our instruments unloaded, the principal came to me and asked if I wanted him to have everybody go outside and come back in again. You see, I had mentioned in the letter I had sent that we would sell the tickets and take up the money and then we would split the proceeds seventy-thirty.

I said, "Absolutely not. You just let them stay right where they are and they can drop their money in this hat when they leave." And I gave him my hat to place at the back of the room.

On the way back after the show, one of the boys said, "Roy, weren't you afraid some of those people wouldn't pay back there?" I told him, "No, sir, I wasn't one bit afraid of that. You know," I said, "you've got to have faith in people." And I'd be willing to bet that we didn't lose one single admission that night. It's the rule I've always conducted my life by—both my show business life and my personal life.

Fortunately there weren't too many unpleasant happenings on the road. That is if you don't call working all day, playing at night, driving home in the wee small hours and then starting all over again at dawn unpleasant. But it really wasn't. It was just something that you did. Road show exposure was important. It was a tough life, and the better known you became, the tougher the life became, primarily because it meant that you traveled farther as your fame increased. But all of the top performers did road shows and I sure wasn't going to be the one to break the tradition.

WSM and David Stone began to book me every night, first in a seventy- or eighty-mile radius, then a little farther out. Mildred and I had a room at the Clarkston Hotel, which was right beside the WSM studio. The hotel is gone now, but in those days I would get back to the hotel late at night or early in the morning, get a few hours' sleep and then get up and go next door to do the morning show on WSM. I would go back to the hotel, and sometimes catch another couple hours' sleep, get up and eat lunch and load up the car. Then the boys and I, and often Mildred, would take off for that night's show.

I decided that I needed to be known as quickly as I could, so I always took somebody along who was already well known. That way their popularity would bring out the people who, in turn, would get to know *me*. It was good for all of us.

Most of the time I took Deford Bailey and Uncle Dave. They were real good at drawing crowds. And the fun we had, particularly with Uncle Dave, made the long hours worthwhile.

Uncle Dave's appearance alone made him interesting, with the gates-ajar collar and the bright tie, the elastic sleeve bands, the pinstripe trousers, the vest with gold watch fob and a black plug hat. He often used the hat to fan the banjo as his gold teeth gleamed his self-described million-dollar smile. But he was a real showman—one of the best I have ever seen—and people in the entertainment world who never got a chance to get acquainted with him really missed something in their lives.

He had a natural sense of humor and his jokes really made any show he was on. A lot of people didn't realize how good his banjo playing was because his jokes were so funny. But he was an outstanding banjo player.

He always brought along three banjos. One of them had a blue ribbon on it, one had a yellow ribbon and the third had a white one, indicating to him which key they were tuned in. So he always referred to them that way: "Hand me that blue-ribbon guitar, son," he would say.

At times we took along Robert Lunn, who was the funniest man I have ever known. He billed himself as the "Talking Blues Man," but I kept him around to entertain *us* more than I did for the sake of the audience. He was full of practical jokes. One night he made sure Uncle Dave wasn't listening. In fact, to make sure, Robert had given Uncle Dave a bottle of Jack Daniels, which was his favorite, saying, "You just go backstage there, Uncle Dave, and have a nip or two out of this

Black Jack bottle while I go out and do some of my talkin' blues numbers." Well, once Uncle Dave was out of earshot, Robert went on stage and did every one of Uncle Dave's jokes. Later when Uncle Dave came out and did the same jokes, they naturally fell flat. He never did know why.

Even though he never drove a car, Uncle Dave insisted that the driver do certain things. I guess he never really trusted cars. I think he always thought of them as a fad, and one that, in time, would pass. He preferred the mule and cart, I suppose because he had all those memories of sitting back and picking the banjo as the mule plodded along. With a car you had to pay attention. He never trusted cars and he had us stop at every railroad crossing, so he could get out of the car and walk up and down the track, making sure there wasn't a train coming.

Uncle Dave had always booked his own shows in the early days and he felt that word of mouth was the best form of advertising, so he went to a town, set up someplace and put on a small free show—a sort of sample—and then let the townsfolks do the rest. He usually had a good crowd for his main show.

But I was a little more positive about my approach. I liked to get there as early as possible before the show and let the people know we were in town. I had gotten a public address system for the car, so we would drive up and down the streets, broadcasting, and letting everybody know we were there. I used every name in the show. The pitch went something like this:

"Ladies and gentlemen and children alike! (Sound familiar?) Tonight at seven o'clock at the Crossville Grade School you'll have the opportunity of a lifetime. Country music, comedy and entertainment for the whole family. A good, clean show for everybody. And it's only fifty cents. Twenty-five for the kids. And you'll see Roy Acuff and his Smoky Mountain Boys. And Uncle Dave Macon, the Dixie Dewdrop, and Deford Bailey, the harmonica-playing wizard, and Pete

The Life and Good Times of Country Music

Kirby with his famous Dobro guitar, and Lonnie Wilson and Jake Tindell. All from the world-famous Grand Ole Opry. Bring the whole family to the best of the Opry right here in Crossville."

I figured that by mentioning everybody's name one of them would appeal to almost everybody. And Uncle Dave really liked it because it reminded him of the circus, which is what I think he always really wanted to do. He never outgrew that childhood dream.

After I became well known, I didn't forget Uncle Dave and Deford and people who had helped me. I took them with me on road shows for years after that.

One of the worst places to play was a gymnasium, because you would say a word and it would bounce off all four walls and then come back when you were a few words ahead. You can imagine how some of the Dobro notes bounced around. You might hear an A still bouncing around eight bars later. At least, it seemed so. But we played all types of places— grammar schools and barns and even outdoors in the summertime, at picnics and fairs where they had built stages for us, and sometimes where they hadn't. I've worked under all sorts of conditions. And I'll tell you, the toughest of all is to stand on the ground and try to entertain an audience, but we did it at times. I've worked under every condition that an entertainer can work under. I've dressed in horse stables and cow barns, and I've worked dairy shows and all types of livestock shows. There were times when one of the boys would get to the punch line of a joke or to the best part of a guitar run and a bull would bellow and completely drown him out. It's tough to get upstaged by an Angus.

But I learned early that you have to work where you have work. You have to bear with it. Fortunately I was brought up that way, so it wasn't too hard to accept when I started doing road shows. That was the trouble with a lot of the boys in those days—and even more so today—they were out there just to sing or to play and they couldn't bend with the circumstances. Man, they weren't brought up in the *enter-tainment* world. They thought everything had to be quiet and perfect and you just went out there and did your song and sat down. That wasn't the life in the early days of country music. You worked day and night, and you worked under every hardship that could be thrown at you. It was the ones who were willing to work that hard that made it. And there were an awful lot of performers that fell by the wayside—performers that really had the talent, but didn't have the determination to stick it out.

It took a whole lot more determination then than it does today. The very fact that we were getting fifty cents for an adult admission in 1940 meant a lot to me. It meant that we were stepping *up*. And the fact that we were playing to full houses meant even more. Because there were a lot of regular Opry performers who weren't playing to full houses, I'll tell you that.

Of course, in all fairness, a lot of them weren't full-time entertainers; possibly they couldn't afford to be. Many of them were farmers, who came in on Saturday night to do the Opry and then had to go back and work that farm all week. They were musicians, all right, and some of them really good ones, but they weren't *entertainers*. There's a world of difference, and as I said, it's determination—and dedication—that makes a musician into an entertainer.

And what with all the traveling so many of us were doing, it's amazing that there weren't more serious accidents. I mean, all of us were dog-tired all the time, and somebody was always going to sleep at the steering wheel. Everybody, that is, except Pete Kirby. He just hated to drive, but we all agreed to take turns, so finally we would shame him into it and he would get behind the wheel and drive for a few miles, and just when he knew somebody was looking at him, he would nod his head forward like he had gone to sleep. Whoever was in the front seat with him would yell at him and tell him to stop before he killed us all. Then somebody else would drive while Pete relaxed. It sure was an effective way to not have to drive.

But occasionally someone really would go to sleep, and there were a few wrecks. Sam McGee was driving one night after they had done a show at Lenoir City and the car went out of control and down over a mountain. His brother Kirk and Sarie and Sally were in the car but they weren't hurt. Kirk dragged Sam out of the car and laid him in the woods while Sarie and Sally crawled back up the hill to the road, where they finally flagged down another car. They took Sam to the doctor to sew up his lip, which had been cut open. Well, he got well, but his lip stayed swollen for weeks. Finally he went to the dentist because a tooth kept bothering him. The dentist accidentally broke open Sam's lip while he was working on the tooth and a piece of gravel fell out. That doctor had sewed up a pebble in Sam's lip.

The Opry was sending out a lot of acts; so were other

Sarie and Sally (Edna Wilson and Margaret Waters), among the first women on the Opry, joined Uncle Dave and me on the tent show circuit. (WSM Archives)

stations. The Monroe Brothers were doing shows as were the Mainer Brothers and Lulu Belle and Scotty and Pee Wee King and the Hoosier Hot Shots. It was an active period for country music.

We all took chances, I suppose, in trying to push ourselves that far, but we knew we had to do it if we wanted to become stars. At least that's the way I felt.

As the boys and I became more popular, just like the pattern I told you about, we traveled farther and farther each week. It finally became more lucrative for me to travel to other states, so I had to give up the morning show on WSM. After that, we loaded up the car right after the Opry and took off for a whole week of public appearances. We looked like a pack of gypsies, but we went to North Carolina and the Virginias and even to Pennsylvania. We went all over. We usually started with a Sunday matinee and then did one-nighters all week, trying to book places that would get us turned around and started back to Nashville by, say, Wednesday night. But there were times when it didn't work, and we might be doing a show in Delaware or Maryland on Friday night and we would have to drive all night to get back to the Opry by Saturday.

Once we were out in the Midwest in the summertime, and it was hot; I mean, it was *hot*. I lay down in the backseat while one of the boys drove down the dusty old unpaved roads, and when I woke up an hour or so later, I thought I was going to choke. I had been sleeping with my mouth open and my tongue was completely covered with dust. I think I would have choked to death if there hadn't been a filling station right down the road. I leaped from the car and grabbed the water hose that was at the gas pumps and washed out my mouth. Then I just ran it over my head. The guy at the station thought I was nuts, I guess.

But we were making more and more money. When I started the road shows from WSM, I offered to pay the boys $22.50 a week, but I always paid them $25—even more when we had a good week. But if anybody ever lost, it was Mildred and me. She almost always traveled with me and she handled the money, and she made sure the boys didn't lose. There were times in those early days when I didn't keep enough to pay for Mildred's and my meals, but we loved it, and we just kept after it until we became winners. It's the absolute secret of my success.

It was a tough life, though it was getting better. We were making more money. But the roads were still bad and places to stay were hard to find. Travel in those days was not an easy thing, especially when you were going as far as the Kansas State Fair, which we did. Roy Acuff and the Smoky Mountain Boys were out there making a name for themselves.

And now there was a Smoky Mountain *Girl*, Rachel Veach. I had added her after Tiny left to go back to Knoxville and she was doing fine, except that I was starting to get some mail about a "girl" traveling with all those men. The people who wrote in didn't realize that Mildred was the best chaperone in the world. All they knew was that it didn't quite fit the image I had created for myself. I really hated the thought of letting Rachel go, because she had a good voice. Besides that, she added a lot to the show with her singing and her banjo.

Mildred and I discussed it and she suggested that I do anything I could to keep Rachel. Everybody in the band liked her. And men in the audience like to see a girl on the stage. Well, Rachel fit the bill. She was eighteen years old when she joined us, and had come from a farm near Peytonville, Tennessee. I think Rachel was as sweet as anybody I had ever met. She was also the most "countrified" person I ever met. And I don't mean that in a bad way at all. It's just that she had never been off the farm. She had never seen an elevator or a Yale lock or a shower. I mean she was really *country,* but that's exactly what I wanted. It came off funny on stage, and yet warm and genuine.

Well, we thought and thought about how we could keep her in the act. Then one day in the car when we were going to

*The Smoky Mountain Boys and
I lay down a few licks. (WSM Archives)*

an appearance, Pete Kirby let out one of his big put-on horse laughs, and that gave me the idea.

"I've got it," I said. "We're gonna make Rachel your sister, Pete."

"I don't need a sister, Roy," he said.

"No, I mean in the act," I said. "Let's see, what'll we call it? I've got it: Rachel and her big bashful brother, Oswald."

"Oswald?" the band said in unison.

"Oswald," I said.

To this day, most people think Pete Kirby's real name is Oswald. He *became* Os. It was the end of the letters and the beginning of one of the most successful acts I ever had. Os dressed exactly like people dressed on the farm—bib overalls and an old hat. The only thing really odd were his shoes. They were a whole lot larger than usual, but not like a clown's. Just big. We always tried to keep some closeness to reality, and we never just came out and made country folks look like fools. Rachel and Os liked to be funny, and they were, on or off the stage. But they never overdid it. Comedy can be overdone, and when it is, it's sad.

I introduced them for the first time in Robbins, North Carolina, and when they came on stage, Os came out first, with Rachel right behind him, just like real-life brothers and sisters on every farm I had ever seen. People loved the simple comedy and easygoing style they had. They were both great laughers and they would cock their heads back and just laugh, the painted gaps in their teeth showing. The audience would roar with them.

Here's a sample of one of their brief but good routines:

RACHEL: "Os, I'm really worried."

OS: "Why you worried, little sister?"

RACHEL: "Well it's my shoulder."

OS: "What's wrong with your shoulder?"

RACHEL: "It hurts like the dickens every time I raise it like this."

OS: "Whyn't you go to the doctor, Rachel?"

RACHEL: "I did."

OS: "Well, did you tell him it hurt you every time you raised it?"

RACHEL: "Yep."

OS: "What'd he say?"

RACHEL: "He said, don't do it."

People in the audience could identify with Rachel and her great big bashful brother, Oswald.

8

They came by bus, horse and buggy, train and foot to record country music.

The recording industry in the United States had gotten off to a booming start. Victor (the Radio Corporation of America, or RCA as we later learned to call it) was much bigger than the rest of the companies in the twenties, so they all tried to come up with some way to catch the leader. Columbia, Edison, and Okeh sold, maybe, three or four million records each per year, while Victor sold one hundred million.

To make matters worse for the smaller companies, along came the depression—Victor was large enough to weather the storm, but a lot of smaller labels failed. Radio really began to cut into record sales. As times got tougher and as radio programing expanded, fewer and fewer people could afford records, because they cost from seventy-five cents to $1.25. That was a lot of money for something you could hear for nothing; providing, of course, that you could come up with the twenty or thirty dollars it cost to buy a radio. But most did, somehow.

Many of the companies started looking around for ways to increase record sales. One of the ways was through what they considered "ethnic" records. Some of the first of these new special-interest records were country, although they weren't listed as such. Victor came to Nashville in the mid-twenties to record eight sides with Deford Bailey. But these records were released as "race" or Negro records.

The first big "break" for country music recording—which certainly was considered "hillbilly" by the New York executives of Victor—came in 1927 in Bristol, whose main street was literally the state line between Virginia and Tennessee. Ralph Peer, a young Victor employee who was searching the mountains for talent, came to Bristol with two engineers and a carload of newfangled recording equipment. It was unusual, if not unique, for anybody to use portable electronic recording equipment, but Peer was convinced that some of the mountain music would sell.

He rented an empty building on State Street, the main street, which really lived up to its name. The building had once been a hat factory, and it was reported that Peer rented it for five dollars a week. He and his engineers worked for a couple of days, getting things ready for what they hoped would be a sea of hillbilly musicians, because the word had gone out to everybody they could contact in the Virginias, Carolinas, Kentucky and Tennessee that they would be recording, and would be signing contracts for more recordings if the artists were good enough.

They built a platform for the recording equipment and covered the walls of the room with blankets they had bought at a textile mill on the way down South. The blankets were to serve as sound baffles in the second-story, makeshift recording studio.

If Ralph Peer had hoped for "stars," his wildest dreams came true. He had run articles in newspapers, telling how much in demand mountain music was throughout the United States and how recording artists from the South had the best opportunity of any musicians in the country. It was certainly the first country music public relations effort.

Well, they came. "They came by bus, horse and buggy, train and foot," Peer said. One of the first was Ernest "Pop"

Stoneman and his family. At that point the A&R man in Peer came out. He let word leak out that not only was Pop getting paid, he was getting *one hundred dollars a day* for recording. That's when the army of people began coming into Bristol.

Most of them never got a contract, and justly, most of them shouldn't have gotten one. But the sessions did flush out some of the rare early talent of country music.

Up in Poor Valley, Virginia—which is exactly what *every* valley in the three- or four-state area really was, it's just that it was the only one to admit it, I guess—Maybelle Carter had teamed up with her cousin A. P. and his wife Sara to form a musical group. They were very popular at church socials and neighborhood get-togethers with their old hymns and gospel songs and ballads. Well, the Carter Family decided to go down to Bristol and have a look at what was going on.

They recorded their first songs on a hot August day. I didn't know anything about it at the time and I probably wouldn't have been there anyway because I was still more interested in baseball than anything else. Most people were. At that time Babe Ruth and Lou Gehrig were in a home-run battle the likes of which nobody had ever seen. It was the year that Ruth hit sixty home runs to win the battle. Calvin Coolidge was President.

In that session, the Carter Family recorded "Bury Me Under the Weeping Willow," "Wandering Boy," "Poor Orphan Child," "Little Log Cabin by the Sea," "The Storms Are on the Ocean," and "Single Girl, Married Girl."

The payment they got was far less than the "hundred-dollars-a-day" rumor had suggested. They were a fine group, right from the beginning. I've heard those records. A. P.'s bass voice sometimes took the lead. Sara specialized on solos and she played the guitar and autoharp. Maybelle was the tenor and guitarist. She flat-picked on bass rather than treble and was associated with what came to be known as "church lick" style. The session was so successful that the Carters were asked to come to New Jersey to record more songs later.

Then Jimmie Rodgers came to town. He was living in Asheville, North Carolina, which was a noted sanatorium for tubercular patients, so he came down out of those hills and recorded "Sleep, Baby, Sleep" and "Soldiers' Sweetheart." He had recorded them earlier but had revised them for the Bristol session.

Jimmie made a little over twenty-five dollars in royalties for "Soldiers' Sweetheart." "Sleep, Baby, Sleep" didn't do a thing, but for some reason the song caught on later that year and became his first big hit. Music critics in New York hailed him as the perfect mixture of folk, hillbilly and Southern Negro blues. He went on to become second only to Enrico Caruso in Victor sales.

The tremendous sales of many country music performers in the late twenties came to a halt almost as quickly as they had been born. The depression again drove people back to their radios. RCA charts show they sold one hundred million records in 1927 but only six million in 1932; still the record companies kept trying. There were portable or makeshift studios set up all over the South.

Uncle Dave told the story of one of the recording sessions. He was to cut some sides and then a black gospel group called the Southern University Quartet was to record. Well, Uncle Dave got to telling them jokes and he had them to the point where all he had to do was look in their direction and they would break up. That didn't matter too much, but he did it while he was singing, and they would have to start all over, which wasn't easy in those days.

The old discs were thick platters, covered with beeswax, and they had some way of chiseling off a layer with a razor blade if a mistake was made. The early machines had a weight like a grandfather's clock, a sort of pendulum, which hung down and turned the gears, which turned the turntable. It was the only way they could be sure that the speed would remain constant, because electrical currents were up and down all the time in those days. The record would move fast and then slow if run by electricity, so they controlled it with weights.

They brought trunks full of waxes—sometimes in various thicknesses—and they didn't like to have to chisel any off because they hoped to have enough sides in each city to record every song from every artist. A stylus cut the wax and they had a sort of suction pump right behind it to pick up the chips or strings of wax. This, along with what they had to "shave," went back to the plant and was remelted for future records.

Well, in this session with Uncle Dave, they were getting quite a collection of shaved wax. For one thing, they always cut a second record of every song for insurance, because the records were very breakable and that way, if something happened, they had a backup. With Uncle Dave they weren't even getting the *first* one. So they tried desperately to get across to the singing group that if they didn't stop laughing at Uncle Dave, there wouldn't be enough wax left for them to record. It quieted them considerably, because they really wanted to record.

But Uncle Dave kept looking back at them, even while he was singing, which meant he wasn't facing the microphone. They only used one mike in the early sessions and they wanted you to sing directly into it. It was located just where it would pick up all the musicians and the singer, so they didn't want anything changed. They had a buzzer, and when it sounded, it meant that something had gone wrong and everybody was to stop playing. After the buzzer had sounded more than Eli Oberstein, who was in charge of the session, could stand, he came over to Uncle Dave and said, "Now Uncle Dave, you're not here for the sake of these boys back there, so let's get something going."

He was right, of course, but he didn't know Uncle Dave. He would have been better off just to keep recording and hope for the best. It was the way Uncle Dave always recorded, just like he wanted to.

"Now, Cap," Uncle Dave said, "I can sing any way I want to and still be heard. I got a lot of git up and go [he meant volume] and I got a smokehouse full of country hams and all kinds of meat to eat up there in Readyville. I got plenty of wood hauled and I don't have to be bossed around by some New York sharpshooter, just to make a few records, because I've done my part on the record-makin' anyway."

He made his point. From then on he did just what he wanted to.

They had all sorts of problems with him. He was an old-time artist and he kept getting closer and closer to the mike, just as he did when he was performing for an audience. So they made a big "X" for him to stand on. They got that problem solved, but they couldn't keep him from stompin' his foot to the beat of the music, so they finally got a pillow for him to put under his foot, so you couldn't hear it on the recording. Besides, his foot was shaking the floor so much that the stylus wouldn't stay on the record. That didn't work, because he said, "Lissen, Cap, that's worse. I mean, I can't hear my foot and it's flat ruinin' my rhythm."

Uncle Dave was one of a kind, and I can still see him swinging his banjo in the air and flashing his gold teeth. He was the ultimate performer, whether he was on stage or recording. And he had the most amazing repertoire of songs of anybody I ever knew.

The thing that turned the record industry around was not the end of the depression, but the discovery of the disc jockey. By the late thirties, radio stations had found out that one person spinning records could save the station a lot of money. A lot of the country stations had many performers who were very popular in their area, so they stuck to live performers—like WSM and WROL and KNOX. But an awful lot of other stations felt that a disc jockey's salary was well worth it. They could let half a dozen musicians go just by playing somebody else's songs on record.

The record companies had traditionally been bitter ene-
mies of the radio stations. I know, it doesn't make sense
today, but it was true then. And when disc jockeys began to
appear, the record companies got up on their hind legs and
fought like mad to keep them from playing the records on the
air. But the Federal Communications Commission didn't
keep things under control then, and the battle was on.
Stations wanted to play records on the air; the record companies didn't want them to.

The battle ended as abruptly as it had started. The record
companies—much to their own amazement—found that
sales were once again booming. So they began to help radio.
The one thing they had feared most—radio—wound up being
their salvation.

Another thing helped the sales of records: Up until then,
records had sold for upwards of one dollar, but Decca lowered
the price to thirty-five cents. Within months, every record
company in the country had to lower its prices to meet
Decca's. By the end of the decade, the record industry was
booming.

It was in this atmosphere that I went to Chicago for my first
recording session. The session began on October 26, 1936, at
the American Record Company (which was later to become
Columbia when it was purchased by the Columbia Broadcasting System). And it was held in an actual studio. I say
"studio," but it wasn't what we think of today as a studio.
There was still only one microphone and there was no sound-
deadening material on the walls. With one mike there was
also no need for a mixing board as we have it today. It was
very primitive equipment, but, you know, as basic as it was,
those old records sounded pretty good.

Recording, in one respect, was more difficult than today.
There wasn't any tape that could be spliced or recorded over,
so if you made a mistake, you had to go back to the very
beginning and start all over again. And, by the time you went
through the number to time it, did the number again to

record it, then did it a third time for breakage insurance—and by that time you might have messed up three or four times—you were plumb wore out.

You could tell in some of my early records, too. The spirit was there, but the voice was wore out.

The Smoky Mountain Boys and I perform while Lew Childre applaudes. This portion of the Opry was referred to as the Prince Albert Show *and aired nationwide over the Blue Network of the National Broadcasting Corporation. (WSM photo by Les Leverett)*

In that first session, I picked half the songs and William Callaway, the A&R man, picked the other half. So that we didn't have any legal squabble, I picked mostly Public Domain (P.D.) songs, songs like "Charmin' Betsy," and naturally, "The Great Speckled Bird." Fortunately for my career, I picked another P.D. song, "Wabash Cannonball."

The first song we did was "Singing My Way to Glory," but Red Jones did the vocal, because I was going to do the fiddle break, and it seemed only fair to let Red sing. You can hear me and the boys talking all through the record. We always did that when we played because it seemed to make us all play better. For instance, when I did the first fiddle break, you could hear the boys urging me on: "Play it, Roy. Play that thing." Then during Clell's Dobro break, you could hear me saying: "Play that thing, Clell. Come on over here and rap on it, boy. Yes siree. Lordy, lordy, lordy. Now sing it, Red." Callaway thought it sounded real good, so he never suggested we not do it.

Since Red preferred popular music, I let him sing the next one, too: "Yes, Sir, That's My Baby." Then Dynamite Hatcher sang "Steamboat Whistle Blues," "Freight Train Blues" and, what surprises most everybody today, he sang the words to "Wabash Cannonball." I didn't do the vocal on it until we recorded again many years later. But I did the background train whistle, because I had learned that when I worked on the railroad as a boy. It's not just because I did it, but I think the train whistle sound is what put the song over. Red, Clell and I sang as a trio on "My Mountain Home Sweet Home" and "Gonna Raise a Ruckus Tonight."

I did the vocals on most of the other songs, including, of course, "The Great Speckled Bird." I knew six verses of "The Bird," and today that would be about twice as many as would be used, but then the songs ran a lot longer, so I had written a few more verses, with the help of the Bible and my father. I used a couple of them in that first recording, and saved some back for a second version of "The Bird."

I sort of cringe when I think of some of the lyrics on some of those songs. For example, I sang the lines *My gal smells just like a billy goat/she's stinkin' just the same* in "Charmin' Betsy." And in "Gonna Raise a Ruckus Tonight" we even used the word "nigger." That was allowed because it had been written that way, although I didn't want to use it, and if I had been a big enough star to have any clout, I sure wouldn't have used it then.

We were about finished with a session when they decided that we needed two more songs, so on the final night in the Knickerbocker Hotel, I wrote some more words to a couple of songs I knew as a youngster but was not allowed to sing at home: "When Lulu's Gone" and "Doin' It the Old-Fashioned

Way." I made them promise me that they wouldn't put my name or any of my boys' names on them in the catalog. They were a little risqué. So they listed the recording artists as being the Bang Boys. It was the only time I ever used a pseudonym. Only a handful of people over the years knew that they were recorded by Roy Acuff and the Smoky Mountain Boys. Until now.

The records weren't released on the American Record Company label because there still was a prejudice against "hillbilly" music, so they were sold through Sears and Roebuck on the Conqueror label. Five and ten cents stores sold them on the Melotone and Perfect labels. Some of the songs eventually got to other subsidiary labels, Vocalion and Okeh, but these songs never got to Columbia, as some of the later ones did.

And you know, they did everything they could to keep people from thinking these were hillbilly records, or even country records. They were listed on the record label and on the paper jackets of the records as "Old Time Singing and Playing" or "Novelty Playing and Singing" or "Singing with Old-Time Playing." One even said, "Sacred Duet by Roy Acuff and Red Jones." We had a ways to go before our type of music was to become respectable.

We recorded once more in Chicago, but things weren't going well between the American Record Company and me. For one thing, I just didn't trust them. I didn't think I was getting the proper royalties. It wasn't until CBS bought them out and they moved the Columbia label to Nashville that I had any faith in them. At that time they brought in one of the finest people I have ever met, Art Satherley. Art was from England but he had a love for country music and he really helped me develop as a recording artist. The first session we did for Art was in Memphis at the Gayoso Hotel. They had rented a large room there and had moved out the furniture so there would be room for the portable recording equipment and the artists. Actually there wasn't enough space for the equipment in the room, so they had to move some of it into the bathroom and cut a hole in the wall for the cables. Naturally they had to go back later and repair the wall, but it served its purpose.

The engineer sat on the toilet, with the recording machine standing on a tripod in the bathtub. I can still see him sitting there, shaving records with a single-edge razor blade on a special turntable. It wasn't exactly what you would call "making it big," at least not by today's standards. But there weren't any standards in those days.

Again we recorded twenty songs in that session. At one time we recorded eight songs in less than two hours, and that figures doing at least two takes of each one. It was so hot during the session that we all stripped down to our waists, and we still just about roasted. I can imagine what someone would have thought if he walked in on that session. I mean, here were musicians, stripped to the waist, playing away while some guy sat on the john, running a recording machine from the bathtub. That session lasted three days.

In later sessions, when it wasn't warm enough in the room, they had to keep the unrecorded discs in a cabinet with a big light bulb inside, so the wax would stay soft enough and not chip while they were recording.

We even recorded once in an old garage in South Carolina. We weren't the only ones recording like this; everybody was doing the same thing. The important thing was—just like it had been with Ralph Peer in Bristol in 1927—to set up somewhere that would attract the musicians, or at least somewhere easy for them to get to. There still wasn't anything permanent to the recording studio.

When we recorded in the garage in South Carolina, they moved a couple of cars out of the way so they could set up the recording equipment, and we set up and got ready to record. In fact, they had already started the recording machine when a woman opened the door and barged right in.

"Where's my car?" she bellowed. "It's s'posed to be fixed."

"'Hold it. Hold it," the engineer said. "Lady, we're makin' a record in here."

"Well, you ain't set no record fixin' my car," she said. "It's been here two days and it ain't fixed yet. Now you call that a record?"

Back to shaving wax.

I guess things like that happened everyplace. I heard of dogs barking and spoiling records and one time an old warehouse actually caught on fire during the final cut of a session. They sent somebody outside to keep the firemen quiet until they finished the session, and then they grabbed all the equipment and instruments and ran.

All the equipment then was portable, and they moved throughout the country, setting up for recording and inviting any talent within, say, fifty miles to come on in and record. They were really there to record some specific groups, but if they could pick up some others while doing it, so much the better. It was a lot easier than taking the talent they wanted to New York or Chicago. And much cheaper. They were on very low budgets.

The engineers often slept in the trucks and then moved right on the next day. The first hint of permanency, so far as recording in Nashville was concerned, came in the early forties. WSM had by then established itself as a major source of network programs, but most of the recordings they used were in the form of transcriptions, which just duplicated about thirty minutes of a radio show. The engineers at WSM learned a lot about recording techniques from the transcriptions, so it was only natural that some of them would start their own recording studio. Carl Jenkins, Aaron Sheldon, and George Reynolds built their "studio" in the slightly dilapidated Tulane Hotel, which was near the WSM studio. The idea was to have a place that traveling A&R men could come to and record their artists. It would save the record companies the trouble of hauling recording equipment all over the South.

The three engineers rented the old ballroom of the hotel, threw up some walls to partition off a recording studio portion, and they bought some pretty good equipment—at least it was as good as, if not better than, anything else any of us had seen. They named it the Castle Studio, because WSM was known as "the Air Castle of the South."

It certainly was a start for the music industry in Nashville. It meant that recording companies were bringing their talent to Nashville, rather than setting up portable studios all over the South. It brought a lot of real talent to Nashville, if only briefly. We all knew that the Castle Studio was only a start. We could see the handwriting on the wall. I think it was Aaron Sheldon's idea first. He had a fantastic set of ears. I mean, he would have made a great chief engineer for any radio station in the country. Or for any recording company.

Owen Bradley and Bob Chester put together big-band arrangements at the studio, and Paul Cohen, the A&R man for Decca, who used WSM's Studio B for sessions with Red Foley, switched to Castle to record early sessions with Ernest Tubb and Kitty Wells.

The studio also was used for radio jingles. In fact, the very first recording done at Castle was a jingle for a local jewelry store, and it featured the voice of Snooky Lanson, a local singer who was later to become the star of the popular radio show *Your Hit Parade*.

Castle Studio was the first step toward the "Music City" title Nashville would become known by. It passed from existence a few years later when the Tulane Hotel was torn down. Even before that, WSM had decided that their moonlighting engineers had better return to full-time recording for WSM. But the die was cast for Nashville as a recording center.

I went by the Tulane Hotel while they were tearing it down, and I thought of some of the wonderful recording that had come out of there. And I also remembered some of the funny anecdotes about the place. The hotels in downtown Nashville were where a lot of the country music history was born. Most of them are gone now.

For example, when they started the disc jockey convention at the Andrew Jackson Hotel, we all went down there, because we knew how much help a DJ can be to a performer who wants to see his records sell.

The convention caught on like wildfire, and the second year there were DJs from all over the country. All over the world, in fact. Record companies rented suites with hospitality rooms. Individual artists came to shake hands and buy drinks. They performed in hallways and on street corners. The whole area was just like Mardi Gras. You could walk around the block and run into half a dozen different people singing to an audience of one. It was like the American Legion and the Shriners had both come to town at once.

There was one time when a guy who was in the hospitality room of one of the record companies fell out of a window. He *fell* out. He hit the canopy below and was as safe as if he had landed in a firemen's net. He crawled over the edge, slid down one of the support poles and walked right back through the lobby, still holding the highball glass he had when he left the room. He had spilled the contents, of course, but he wasn't long in getting back to the room for a refill.

As he walked in, all ruffled up, the man he had been talking to when he disappeared was in about as bad shape as he was. "Where the hell'd you go?" he asked.

"I jesh stepped out for a breath of fresh air," he slurred.

9

During a storm you could hear the wham! wham! wham! of the roustabouts' hammers as they drove the stakes deeper, so the tent show could go on.

Where the medicine shows left off, the tent shows took over in the small and large cities of the South. They brought a touch of vaudeville to many towns that otherwise never would have had it. In the beginning, tent shows came to the towns by horse-drawn wagon, but by the forties they arrived by car and truck, so they got to more towns. My father had told me about a tent show he saw years before that included everything from trained bears to Irish tenors.

It seemed only natural then that I move my traveling show to the big top. I guess I never got over the medicine show days. It had been a pleasant experience for me and I thought that the tent show would be the same thing. For one thing, I liked playing to large crowds, and many of the schoolhouses and courthouses had such limited space that we couldn't get that many people in. So it also seemed like an economically good idea.

Country shows of any kind always drew pretty good crowds because farm boys, for example, looked for any reason to get to the city. The drab, work-all-day life on the farm got old in a hurry, and besides that, there has always been some excitement to city life for a boy—or a man or woman, for that matter—who grew up on a farm. The city, no matter how small, was a symbol to them of bright lights and excitement. It also was the center of corruption to some. But it meant excitement, nevertheless.

In addition to that, there were scores of farm boys who had moved to the city to work in the industrial plants and in the textile mills and on the railroads, and any contact they could have with the country was important to them. Country music was this contact. So, armed with these beliefs, I began thinking tent show.

Jamup and Honey, who had been a successful Opry comedy team, had found a big tent—it was 85 by 180 feet, so it would hold a lot of people. Uncle Dave and my boys and I decided to go along, and it turned out to be just like a circus. Uncle Dave loved that. He had finally made the canvas and sawdust trail.

We sent a "paper man" out in advance to put up posters and signs. By the time we got to town, there were posters on every telephone pole in the area, and in every store window. We gave every store owner a free ticket if our man could put up a sign. Our advance man would also find a good location for us to put up the tent, which was usually down by the railroad tracks, where the rent was cheaper. And, just like the regular road show technique, we took ads in the local newspaper and on the radio, planning to have an ad running over two Sundays before we got there. We bought the town, police and all.

It was a wonderful experience, because people could come to the tent in their work clothes, or they could dress up, whatever they wanted to do. They could just come down and sit around and enjoy the show. And it was a "show," not a parade of stars like the road shows later became. We didn't depend on a dozen celebrities to get a crowd, we counted on our own good names. And on entertainment. I guess that was the key, we *entertained* people. Sure it was work, but it paid off in large crowds, because our reputation always preceded us. People knew that they were going to get their dollar's worth. It's all changed today because performers don't really get to know show business. Maybe they can stand up and sing a song or play a solo on an instrument, but that's it. There's very little show business in people today. I mean, the boys and girls today can't hold an audience like we could back then. Why, I've seen Uncle Dave hold an audience for an hour and a half, all by himself. And he left them wanting more.

It was no trouble at all for any of the groups back then—at least, any of the successful groups—to hold an audience for

Uncle Dave Macon (seated) and I enjoy a Saturday Evening Post *poster about the Grand Ole Opry. (WSM photo by Les Leverett)*

an hour or two. We would do some sad songs, then break them loose with some comedy and then some lively songs, and maybe more sad songs. It was entertaining, and we played on every emotion the crowd had. When they left the tent, they felt like they had been somewhere. The shows had a lot of character.

We did it every night, not just on weekends as they do today. We worked all over, and then got back to Nashville on Saturday night for the Opry, and then left again on Sunday; sometimes right after the Opry on Saturday night if it was a long trip.

I was so pleased with tent shows that the next year I bought my own tent. And I'll tell you right now, it was a big operation and a lot of work. For one thing, we had a fleet of trucks; one to haul the tent, one for the sound equipment and light plant, one for the folding chairs and supplies, and a fourth one that hauled the cook tent and the supplies for that. It took a pretty good crew of roustabouts to put up the tent and they had to be fed. They slept in the tent most of the time, but there wasn't a set time for them to sleep. They would tear down the tent right after the show and go on to the next town, which was usually thirty or forty miles away. It was always late when they got there, so they would put up the cook tent and sleep in that at times and then put up the main tent the next morning. At times they slept on the ground.

The roustabouts were afraid of fire and wind, and lots of times when a storm came up during a show—as it often did in the summertime—you could hear the beat of their mallets striking the tent stakes. Wham! wham! wham! And I knew they were out in the storm, putting the stakes in deeper. They were concerned, and that made us all a little uneasy. It didn't do much for one's stage presence.

We stayed in small hotels or tourist homes, wherever we could find rooms. There weren't any motels then; there were what people called tourist courts, which were a series of small, one-room cabins, but they, too, were scarce.

Some of the booking was done through WSM's Artist Service Bureau, and there were times that they used us as guinea pigs. They would send us out to an area where there hadn't been any country acts before, or at least not for a long time. They wanted to see how we did. Since we always played to a full house everywhere, it made us a good barometer for other acts. Even though we filled the tent all the time, there were some places where I came away and reported back to Nashville, "This is no place for country music," because I knew that some of the other acts just wouldn't go over there.

We started out in Georgia in early spring and worked our way north, up through the Carolinas and Virginias, up to Ohio. And then we worked down through the Southwest to Oklahoma and Texas by fall. It was all over in late fall and then we went back to the regular circuit of working every other type of arena, some of them small, some large, which was uncertain, at best. Under the tent, we knew what to expect. We could get about twenty-five hundred people *in* the tent, and by "sidewalling" it we could add another five hundred or six hundred. Sidewalling meant actually propping up the side walls with poles and tying them off with ropes and, by doing that, extending the area. People stood under these flaps, which had become their roof. We sidewalled the tent almost every night.

And we drew crowds. Big crowds. Once in South Carolina, a preacher who was having a tent revival told his congregation, "Well, I know everybody will want to hear Brother Roy tomorrow night, so we won't have any service tomorrow." We had some Monday night crowds—that's traditionally the worst night in show business—that were bigger than the Saturday night crowds at the Opry. We got to the point where we not only sidewalled the tent, but also had them lined up outside, standing on their tiptoes, straining to get a glimpse of the entertainers.

We learned to like summer and the tent, because winter often brought problems. Since we were venturing way out by now, we got into some pretty bad weather. We got stranded in Wyoming one night while on our way to Denver, Colorado. My car slid into a snowbank, and the two other cars carrying the rest of our group slid right in behind us. The snow was halfway up to the doors when a snowplow came by and plowed us all completely under. I lowered the window and scraped enough snow away so I could get the door open and get out. I scraped more snow away and got the doors open on the other cars, so somebody could get out and help me at least partially uncover the cars, so they could be seen. Then I got back inside to wait.

It was a couple of hours before anybody got through the mountain pass and when the first vehicle came, it was a bread truck with chains on. Right up there in the Rockies. He pulled to a stop, slid open his door and tossed us several loaves of bread to eat until help came.

When the blizzard stopped, some of us walked down the mountain to where some other cars were stranded and we helped push them out. Then they came back up and helped us. Our three cars got into Buffalo, Wyoming, early the next morning, and I stopped at a whiskey store and got a bottle of whiskey for each car, just in case we got stranded again.

We never made the Denver appearance and, you know, it was the only one I ever missed in my life. I had sent a telegram from Wyoming, but I learned later that they had a full house anyway. They never did tell the papers or radio stations that we were stranded and wouldn't make it. They went ahead and used my name and filled the house. Then, at showtime, they announced it to the audience and went on with a local country music group. The booking agent never even said, "Thanks, Roy, for the use of your name," or "We're glad you didn't freeze to death," or anything.

There were many nights that we traveled all night to get to a show, played to a capacity house and entertained our hearts out, and there almost never was a promoter or booking agent who ever said, "Thanks for the extra effort, Roy." Not to mention the fact that we filled his house when most acts didn't. There was one promoter up at a park in New Hampshire who came up after the show and said, "Roy, here's your money. And, by the way, I put in an extra two hundred fifty dollars because of the big crowd you drew. We really appreciated it." And I appreciated that, too. It was the only time it ever happened.

But we kept plugging away. Robert Lunn said one night, "If you work for Roy Acuff, you need a lunchpail and a miner's lamp, 'cause you eat in the back of the car and you never stop."

Traveling with two or three cars got to be so much of a problem that I had a special car built for us. Actually it was a sort of bus—more like the airport limousines you see today. It was a white 1940 Ford four-door sedan, which had been stretched to eight doors. It had a big luggage rack on top for the instruments and a fold-down rack behind the trunk for any overflow luggage or instruments that wouldn't fit on top. With the new "bus" we could haul everybody in one car and it made life a whole lot easier.

Robert looked at it and said, "Sure hope we don't get stuck in a snowbank with this one, Roy. What with the white color, hell, they'd never find us. Wouldn't be nothing left come spring but a pile of bones and guitar strings."

But even in the winter, we got to playing some big auditoriums, with some audiences even bigger than the tent show's. It was nothing for us to play to an audience of five thousand on a Monday night in, say, a park in Pennsylvania. A *Monday* night.

It was a long way from the one-room schools and the dream of the hundred-dollar house.

I used a lot of different performers in my road shows for one reason or another. I tried to take Uncle Dave and the Delmore Brothers and Deford along, and Sam and Kirk McGee and Clyde Moody, because they were good performers. But no

The band and I with the stretched-out Ford that hauled us around the country in the forties. Standing, from left to right: Uncle Dave Macon, Dorris Macon, myself, Pete Kirby, and George D. Hay (with Huspakena, his horn). Kneeling, from left to right: Lonnie (Pap) Wilson, Jess Easterday, and Rachel Veach. (WSM photo by Les Leverett)

Getting top billing over Ronald Reagan at the Palace Theater in New York. (Roy Acuff Collection)

matter who I carried along, I made sure they were performers who would entertain any audience. Jimmy Riddle joined my band about that time, and he added a lot.

The one exception to the rule was Robert Lunn. Oh, he was talented enough, but I kept him around just for the morale of our own people. He entertained the crowds very well, but he kept us in stitches.

Robert was walking down the street in Little Rock with Jimmy Riddle one day and Robert took Jimmy by the arm and whispered to him, "Jimmy, Sam's walking up right behind you. Now, you just keep walking and when he gets close, you spin around and you scream at him, right at the top of your lungs. It'll scare the hell out of him." Well, Jimmy walked along and in a minute he whirled around and yelled WAAAHHHHHHH so loud you could hear it two blocks away. And you know, it wasn't Sam at all. It was some complete stranger. Robert was right, it scared the hell out of him, but he had never seen Jimmy before at all. Jimmy stammered and stuttered and tried to explain, but the man just wanted to get out of there.

And another time Robert was holding informal—and fake, of course—auditions in the alley beside the Ryman Auditorium. Well, people had come from all over the country to see the Opry and a lot of them had hopes of someday getting on stage themselves. So Robert waited until one walked by who had a guitar or a fiddle and he would tell him that he was in charge of the Opry program and was "looking for new talent." He had some of those poor boys doing everything in that alley but standing on their heads.

One night he had this poor country boy playing the guitar, and he asked him if he could sing. "Sure can," the boy said, and then he was singing and picking. Then Robert asked if he could dance. "Well, I can do a buck dance," the boy said. "Okay," Robert said. "Go ahead." "You mean, while I'm singin' and pickin'?" "Sure," Robert said. So this boy was singing and picking and dancing like mad when George Morgan walked up.

"Robert, you oughta be ashamed of youself," he said. "I mean, look at the boy up there just working his butt off."

Robert looked at him and said, "George, if you wasn't such a big star already, I'd have you up there doin' the same thing."

And he probably would have. Robert was very persuasive. And believable.

You just don't see people like Robert Lunn anymore. Today it's a dog-eat-dog world, and nobody has much fun. Everybody always tried to give Robert some of his own medicine, but he was a pro when it came to practical jokes, and it was next to impossible to get one on him.

I had a group of girl singers one time who had suffered through about half a dozen of Robert's practical jokes and were determined to get even. So one of the girls came up to Robert and told him that she had this beautiful girlfriend who wanted to meet him. "I mean to tell you," she said, "she's beau-ti-ful, Robert, and she'll be at the corner of Fourth and Main tomorrow afternoon at four o'clock. Now don't you stand her up, because she's a big fan of yours and she wants to show her appreciation. She will be wearing a red dress. Now don't forget, you stop the first girl you see with a red dress, and that'll be her."

Well, Robert could see through that because he had done the same thing to a dozen male artists who thought they were ladykillers. He had them standing on street corners all over Nashville. So Robert came to me and said, "Roy, those girls are tryin' to set me up, and I need your help." Well, I was always in for a good practical joke, so I helped him. We knew this cashier at a drug store right around the corner from Fourth and Main, so we went over there and I said to her, "Lucille, we need your help to play a joke on some friends. If you'll meet Robert here tomorrow at four o'clock, I'll give you ten dollars. All you have to do is walk by, and he'll stop you and then you just walk down the street with him. Just out of sight." Well, she agreed and I gave her the ten dollars. "Oh," I said, "I forgot. Have you got a red dress?" She said she did and that she would wear it to work. She was going to have to take time off from work, but I assured her that it would only take five minutes and she said she'd use her coffee break for it.

On the next afternoon, the girls were hiding so they could see the corner. Robert walked up a couple of minutes before four and waited on the corner. They started to giggle. In a couple of minutes Lucille came walking down the street, wearing the red dress, and Robert stopped her. The girls couldn't believe their eyes. They could see from where they were, but they couldn't hear what was said. All they knew was that this stranger in a red dress walked up, Robert stopped her, and they walked off down the street, arm in arm. It cured them of practical jokes, since they thought he'd picked her up. We never told the girls any different.

It was during this period that I added another girl to the show, one who followed a tradition of comics on the Opry. Or at least she tried to follow the tradition, which meant she would do anything to make an audience laugh—even fall off the stage if necessary. At times, some of the performers dressed to extremes; well, not to the point of putting mops on their heads, but they would take a character, who was always somebody they had seen—maybe somebody in their home-town, or somebody they had met in their travels—and they would build a character around that person. They never tried to belittle the country-person image—all of us were too sensitive to ever do that—but they portrayed the way that person dressed or talked.

Sarah Ophelia Colley, who was a well-educated, fashionable young woman, had taught dancing for a few years before she decided that she wanted to do comedy. Stand-up comedy. She created a small-town, man-hungry old maid named Minnie Pearl, and she came to the Opry as that character.

Fancy clothes and blacked-out teeth—along with a barrage of country humor—made Roland Sullivan as Oscar (left) and John Sullivan as Lonzo Opry favorites for years. (WSM Archives)

The character of Minnie Pearl was supported with a host of unseen friends and relatives, all as outlandish as Minnie, and most from the imaginary town of Grinder's Switch.

After a few Opry appearances, she asked if I could use her in my traveling show. She really wanted experience and everybody had told her she would get more traveling with my road shows than with anybody. I told her to come along. She worked for me for three months, and I had some grave concerns about her performance.

For one thing, the role was not really her. She was so well-educated and proper, and I didn't think she was ready to turn loose and be a comic. At that time it was very hard for any true Southern lady to let go and be a fool. I told her, "Minnie, you've got some talent, and your material is real good, but you've got to turn loose. You've got to be a fool, Minnie. I mean, you're out there to entertain people, so you've got to give them a show."

She tried. Lord, how she tried. But you could tell that she was torn between what she was trying to do and her other desire—to be a serious actress. It's a long step from the role of a dramatic actress to that of a fool, and she was having a hard time making the total commitment. I told her that if she wanted to be a comic, she had to be a comic, and that if she wanted to be a serious actress, then she had to be a serious actress. "Let yourself go, Minnie," I kept telling her.

But her timing was off. At times, she didn't wait for the people to get the joke, and you've got to give an audience time. If it's funny, they'll get it. But she couldn't wait. She was working much too fast. She would go out there and hit them with a dozen good jokes and maybe they wouldn't get half of them because she was already into another one while they were still working on the joke before. Then she would come off the stage and cry.

This is hard to believe today when you listen to Minnie Pearl work, but I finally had to go to her and say, "Minnie, it's just not working out for you. I mean, my show. You're going to make a good performer someday, but this isn't the place to do it." She knew I was right and, thank God, we remained friends. In fact, she's one of the dearest friends I have ever had in my life.

Her career got a real boost later when she got the chance to do the Camel Caravan show for the armed forces. It was just exactly what she needed. There were so many shows to do and she got so much exposure and so much experience so fast that she completely forgot about wanting to become a serious actress. When I saw her work a couple of years later, I just stood there and beamed. I was so proud of her. She was funny. Real funny, and her timing was perfect. Sarah Ophelia Colley had *become* Minnie Pearl, and the world of country music is much better for it.

"Minnie," I said, "You've given yourself over to the act.

Rod Brasfield teamed up with Minnie Pearl to form the most successful Opry comedy team ever. (WSM photo by Les Leverett)

That's exactly what I always wanted you to do. You're acting crazy and, you know, that's what they want. You're really giving people a show, Minnie."

The boys and I went to Hollywood in the early forties to make some movies. That's right, we went there to make *movies*. If anybody had told me earlier that I would some day be a movie star, I would have had him locked up. But I made eight movies, five for Republic Studios and three for Columbia. Most of them had a Western theme, but one, *Grand Ole Opry*, featured Uncle Dave and the Solemn Old Judge.

Uncle Dave and the Judge took a train out so they got there long before we did. In fact, Uncle Dave sent word that he absolutely had to have a country ham. So I carried one out to him, had it all packed up in a wooden crate and everything, and we took that thing all the way to California. Well, he ate the whole thing during the course of the filming. "Just don't trust this California food," he said.

The whole Hollywood incident was stange to all of us. For one thing, we were used to simple, everyday people and events. There was all this make-believe atmosphere to everything out there—and it wasn't just the movie sets. The people were about as phony as the backdrops. And they treated us like freckle-faced stepchildren. Real country boobs, they thought. It wasn't until my boys got into a poker game with some of the movie production people that they began to look on us as equals. My boys took them for every cent they had. Just as they were cleaning up the last cent of Hollywood money in the game, Uncle Dave came along and said, "Looks like you fellers just got a taste of good ol' Southern hospitality."

"Whatta ya mean, Southern *hospitality?*" one of them asked.

"Well," Uncle Dave replied, "you still got your cameras, ain't ya?"

After that, they treated us all with a lot more respect. In fact, Uncle Dave used to entertain all of them by the hour. He would sit and tell stories and the director would have to make him stop so they could get on with the filming. By the time he left to go back to Nashville, he had quite a following in Hollywood.

I took him to the train station because we were going to stay to make some more films. As he boarded the train, Uncle Dave said, "Roy, I sure would appreciate it if you could bring that crate the ham was in when you come back. It'll sure make a good nest for one of my chickens."

I got to where I enjoyed making movies. And the people said I didn't do all that bad at acting, either. Most of the films were Westerns and I had a lot of lines to learn and some

A scene from one of my movies, Night Train to Memphis. (*Roy Acuff Collection*)

stunts to work out. I didn't have a double so I had to take all the falls myself and I had to fake a lot of fights. That was unnatural to me because I wasn't used to *faking* a fight. I wasn't used to losing one either. But I lost a lot and I didn't even get the girl in any of the films. I figured this good-guy stuff wasn't all it was cracked up to be.

But I did get to sing in all the films, and the boys got plenty of chances to play their brand of good country music. They sounded so good, in fact, that the other actors and the people on the set often asked us to play and sing after we had finished filming. The routine went something like this: Get up at five A.M., go to the studio and start filming at daybreak, film all day and sing and fight and ride horses. Then at the end of the day, we picked up our instruments again and gave a concert for everybody in the film company. Our evening concerts got so popular that people from other movies were coming around to hear them.

When we had any time off, which wasn't often, we played at some local clubs. And on weekends we did a network portion of the Opry direct from Hollywood. It was a long way from the Clinch Mountains.

When we finished our eighth movie, it was time to return to the hills. I sort of hated to go, but, at the same time, we all knew that it really wasn't our atmosphere—our "bag," they'd say today. So we packed up the car and we headed home. The last thing we tied on top of the car was Uncle Dave's wooden crate. Somehow, it seemed like an appropriate gesture to start us back toward reality.

10

*Ernest Tubb and Chet Atkins and Hank
Snow and a lot of others were headed
for the Opry.*

The basic philosophy of the country musician didn't change,
even though times were changing. The country's economy
had outlasted the depression. And another interesting thing
was happening; country music was outlasting the prejudice
that had plagued it since the earliest days. At least in most
places.

When I first came to Nashville nobody had a bank account
or any insurance or any property. Most of them still didn't in
the forties. The only thing they had was a basic country
philosophy. They didn't worry about anything; money, a place
to live, jobs, anything. I mean, if you told one of them, "Boy,
you're gonna lose your job if you don't stop doing that," more
than likely he would answer, "Well, that's okay, Roy. I was
lookin' for a job when I found this one."

There was a lot of migration from job to job and radio
station to radio station. And from recording company to
recording company, but then I guess that's what made country music and country musicians different. It's this transient
philosophy. I think it's what made the music so casual, and
maybe it's why it was finally being accepted. Whatever it was,

it made life a lot more pleasant not to be treated as a second-class citizen.

I was getting so much mail from places like New York and Chicago—and most of them were asking to buy sheet music for my songs, especially "The Wabash Cannonball" and "The Bird"—that I figured there must be a market out there for the words as well as the records. I decided to publish a little songbook and sell it on public appearances and over the air. I asked Harry Stone, who was station manager for WSM, if I could do it and he said, "Sure, but you'll have to pay for the air time."

We agreed on a fifteen-minute show, the first fifteen-minute spot after ten P.M. on the Opry. A perfect time. It would cost me eighty-five dollars and I would supply the talent. Sounded like a whale of a deal to me.

The boys and I picked out our most requested songs, which were "Wabash Cannonball" and "The Great Speckled Bird," naturally. But the list of songs I was going to put in the book also included some of the songs I had written, like "The Precious Jewel" and "The Great Shining Light." Then there were a lot of others, like "Gabriel's Trumpet," "Lonely Mound of Clay," "Weary River," "Just to Ease My Worried Mind," "A Vagabond's Dream," "That Beautiful Picture," "The Old Age Pension," "Mother's Prayer Guides Me," "Behind Those Walls of Gray," and "My Radio's Dialed to Heaven on High." The songbook would cover the whole range of songs we played.

In addition to having a short history of Roy Acuff and the Smoky Mountain Boys, it had four postcard-size photos of the boys and me in action, one of the stretched Ford "bus," and one of me playing the fiddle. The whole thing folded up like an accordion. The idea of the songbook's being that size was that it could be folded up and put in your pocket to take to church or school or wherever. And it could be used as a self-mailer, because there was a space on the front for an address, just like the folding postcard packets you could get in almost

Onstage on the Ryman Auditorium. The backstage congestion amazed newcomers to the Opry, but the acts were always right on schedule. (WSM photo by Les Leverett)

any city, showing various scenes of that particular town. Besides, being that size I could get them printed for a nickle each. I found out from the post office that it could be mailed for one cent.

I turned in the copy and the photographs to the McQuitty Printing Company in Nashville two weeks before I went on the air to make the first Saturday night announcement. We did our first show and I started the pitch for the songbook. They cost twenty-five cents each. Well, I had told the printer to run off "about five thousand," feeling that that would hold us for a while, but by Wednesday of the next week, WSM had already received orders for well over ten thousand. They went plumb nuts. I mean, they were afraid the whole thing was going to fall back in their laps, so they gave me six assistants to help me get them mailed out, just so they could get the whole thing out of the station. I rented a trailer right next to the one Mildred and I were living in and we went into the mail-order business. And I went back to the printer and told him to just keep the presses running until I said "stop."

Os and Jimmy Riddle carried the quarters to the bank in wheelbarrows, where they were counted by machine. By the end of the first two months we had sold well over one hundred thousand songbooks, and before it was over, I guess we must have sold over a million of them.

If I were to credit my success to any *single* thing, it would be the songbook. For one thing, it allowed me to travel better. While a lot of the other acts were out there having car trouble and arriving late, all worn out, or not arriving at all, we were now traveling in Cadillacs. We had no more car trouble. And we wore better clothes and played better instruments. I mean, we had a real class act.

It took a lot of money, even then, to keep a show on the road—just keeping the cars running, buying gas and hotel rooms and costumes, not to mention salaries. And the rest of the boys didn't have the cushion I had with the songbook to fall back on if a calamity struck, and calamity in those days could come in the form of a blown engine, or almost any unforeseen expenditure.

My boys would sell songbooks at the Opry and at personal appearances, and I gave them a cut. They were making as much as fifty dollars a night from that alone. We were all pretty happy about the whole deal, because it enabled me to do a lot of things that other performers either never thought of or couldn't afford to do. For instance, instead of sharing the cost of a big auditorium with somebody else, I would just buy out the whole place myself. That way I didn't have to share the profits with anybody—no other group or promoter or booking agent. The profits were all mine.

We even rented the Ryman Auditorium from time to time in the middle of the week. We would advertise on radio and in the newspaper and then we would fill the house. Simple. Nobody else was doing much of that sort of thing in the early forties. In fact, I can point to one thing with a great deal of pride: I have never played a loser in my life. There are a lot of people who can't say that. And I think it all came from taking ideas like the songbook and using the proceeds properly to bring more money in.

My lifestyle hadn't changed all that much, just because all of a sudden I had money. Oh, I lived well enough, but I didn't run out and buy some fancy mansion and just throw it away like so many performers did later when money really started to roll in. The only reason we drove Cadillacs was that they were dependable. It wasn't to make an impression on anybody. In fact, I had a slight disagreement with the local Cadillac dealer after buying several cars there, so I switched to Chryslers after that. I just wanted a big car because of the comfort.

I can remember the day Ernest Tubb arrived at the Opry. He drove up in one of those old Chevys with "knee action," the kind that looked like they were going down the hill all the time. It was black with yellow wheels. Justin was with him and he was about three feet tall at the time. We all had heard about Ernest, because he was so popular in Texas, so when he got out of the car everybody knew who it was. He was tall and skinny, and with the fancy Western duds, he fit the bill of a Texan just like he had come from Central Casting. He also fit the bill of a star. He just had that quality about him.

Ernest's idol was Jimmie Rodgers and the story was that Jimmie's widow had given him a lot of help because everybody had said he sounded a lot like her late husband. I never thought that. I always thought Ernest sang just like Ernest Tubb, which was plenty good enough. He said that he first heard Jimmie's records when he was thirteen and he would walk twelve miles into town just to hear them. He spent five dollars for a guitar and taught himself to play from an instruction book. He practiced and practiced until at times his fingers were bloody, but he learned to play. And he learned to yodel.

Ernest spent a few years playing for a dollar or two a night in oilfield honkytonks, before he finally landed a job on a Beaumont, Texas, radio station. One day when he was working in San Antonio, Ernest decided to see if Jimmie's widow was in the phone book. He didn't really expect to find her, but he did. He called the number and told her of his admiration for Jimmie and asked if she would happen to have an autographed picture of his idol that he could have. Mrs. Rodgers invited him over and then spent three hours visiting and listening to him sing. She didn't think he sounded like her Jimmie, but she was impressed with his talent and with his sincerity. Then she gave him not only an autographed photo, but also Jimmie's guitar, for which she had turned down offers of up to three-thousand dollars. And she began to help Ernest with his tours and with a recording contract.

He wasn't an immediate success, despite a lot of recording and even a Hollywood movie role as a singing cowboy. In fact, it wasn't until the summer of 1941, when he recorded "Walking the Floor Over You," that people everywhere began to take notice. And who could ignore a song with lyrics that told of walking the floor all night, unable to sleep a wink. Ernest went on to sing about praying while his heart was breaking. The song was a natural and an immediate hit for Decca, selling more than three million copies.

The Opry beckoned for Ernest but he didn't think he was ready, so he came to Nashville with some reluctance. That didn't last long. He was an immediate hit. He became an instant Opry favorite. And I think he summed up his singing and his attitude toward country music as well as anybody ever had:

"I don't read music and I'd fight the man who tried to teach me. I don't care whether I hit the note right or not. I'm not looking for perfection of delivery—thousands of singers have that. I'm looking for individuality. I phrase the way I want to. I sing the way I feel like singing at the moment."

Ernest went right back to the road, where he still is today—sharing his time with people all over the country and with Opry listeners on Saturday night. He's a little different from some of the rest of us in that he's primarily a club entertainer, and he uses a set of drums. Although he didn't have drums with his Texas Troubadors that first night, he did have an electric guitar, and the crowd loved it.

Crowds everywhere were starting to love not just Ernest's music, but all music. And record sales reflected it. In turn, more good music was being written. Another Texan who was starting to attract a lot of attention was Bob Wills. Bob was probably the first to combine basic *country* music with Western. He bridged the gap a long time before most people thought it was possible. He took the fiddle, guitar, and banjo and added a steel guitar, bass, drum, trumpet, trombone, and even piano. The Texas Playboys were the band with a beat, and Bob was referred to as the "Daddy of Western Swing."

But again it was a single hit that called the nation's attention to him. Bob wrote and recorded "San Antonio Rose," and I doubt that any other country record ever sold so fast. He would have made a great Opry regular, but the lure of the

Ernest Tubb, truly one of the all-time great country singers. (WSM Archives)

Southwest was greater to him. He made his living mostly from dance halls.

But there were a lot of other stars who were headed for the Opry. Chet Atkins, for one, had followed my pattern almost exactly. He was born in Luttrell, Tennessee, which was only a few miles from Maynardville in the Clinch Mountains. And he started on WNOX in Knoxville. As a fiddler. That's right, Chet was a fiddler when he started. It's probably good for the music world that he switched to the guitar, because he was to become one of the greatest guitarists who ever hit the Opry stage, or any stage, for that matter.

Chet also quickly proved to the world that he had talent as a writer. With Boudleaux Bryant, one of the great songwriters, he wrote "How's the World Treating You?" It couldn't miss with lines like *I've had nothing but sorrow/Since you said we're through/There's no hope for tomorrow/How's the world treating you?* And it didn't.

Another great who was destined for Opry stardom came from, of all places, Nova Scotia. Hank Snow had been kicked out of his house when he was fourteen, so he signed aboard a fishing schooner, where he entertained the sailors with his five-dollar guitar and the songs of (you guessed it) Jimmie Rodgers. After that he worked all over Canada, playing schoolhouses and places like we were playing in the South. Ernest and Hank kept the fire and the legend of Jimmie Rodgers alive for many years.

You can see the pattern. Country musicians from all over were plugging away, with one eye on their fans and, no matter where they were, the other eye on Nashville. And the Opry was keeping an eye to the hinterlands, as well. The minute someone came up with a hit song, the Opry officials were sharp enough to try to get him or her to the Ryman Auditorium to perform. It's no wonder that the Grand Ole Opry remained the favorite Saturday night entertainment of the whole country.

Hank Snow's hit "Movin' On" carried him to stardom

Wilma Lee and Stoney Cooper came out of the hills of West Virginia. They were among the best loved "mountain style" artists in the history of country music. (WSM photo by Les Leverett)

throughout the continent and on the Opry as well. The lyrics brought one of the all-time favorite subjects of country music to the limelight—trains. In the song, an eight-wheeled train rolling down the track is a way of moving on and leaving troubles and heartache behind.

All of this success brought musicians to Nashville from every hollow and most of the towns in the country. There wasn't enough work for them, so pretty soon every restaurant and every hotel in Nashville had an aspiring musician washing dishes or carrying suitcases. And they were standing on every street corner and walking every street, picking and singing.

With all the outstanding music and the big stars, Nashville's recording industry naturally began to boom. The Brown Brothers opened a studio near the corner of Fourth and Church streets and RCA moved its recording efforts there. RCA later moved to Fourth and Union to share a studio with the Presbyterian Church for a while before finally building its own recording studio, becoming the first recording company to have its own recording facilities in Nashville.

My band in the late forties. Standing, from left to right: Jimmy Riddle, myself, Helen Lecroix, Inez Lecroix, Ann Lecroix, Benny Martin, and Joe Zinkam. Seated: Oral Rhodes and Pete (Oswald) Kirby. (WSM photo by Les Leverett)

Capitol Records became the first to locate its country music director in Nashville, followed shortly by Mercury Records. Groups of all types—including Woody Herman and Ray Anthony with their big bands—were recording in the Ryman Auditorium, because they all loved the acoustics there.

Tape recorders were starting to replace the old discs, and the whole city was going wild with recording. Owen Bradley opened a studio at Second and Lindsley. Many of the major labels were recording in Nashville by the mid-forties, but independents were starting to spring up as well. Jim Bulleit

was the first of the successful independents with his Bullet
Records. Their first big hit was a popular song recorded by
Francis Craig, "Near You." Other big Bullet hits included one
by Bob Wills's brother, Johnnie Lee Wills, called "Rag Mop."

Francis Craig had been around Nashville for years as a
hotel band leader and his hit record proved to the rest of the
world that there was enough recording talent around Nashville, whether country or pop, to make it worthwhile as a
recording center. Side men sprang from the restaurants and
motels. Those labels that hadn't been in the city before were
suddenly present.

*Owen Bradley was a studio musician and nationally known band leader
before becoming one of Nashville's most important recording executives.
"Bradley's Barn" was the pride of Nashville recording studios for years.
(WSM Archives)*

Owen Bradley built a studio for Decca, from an old lodge in South Nashville, but a dispute with the landlord forced him to move to Hillsboro Village, where he stayed for quite a while before building his Quonset Hut studio back in Nashville.

In the beginning, acoustics were terrible in the studios. In fact, they had this circular feeling, which was awful, but then nobody knew anything about acoustics, so nobody complained. Eventually, somebody got some deadening material and, little by little, the studios all became "dead." It was the beginning of a period when you didn't want the room to add anything to a record. Today, when you can add one track at a time, and there is so much overdubbing, you want to control everything as it goes on, so a lot of people still want a dead room. They don't want five or six instruments to run together in a hodgepodge.

The fifty-thousand-watt WSM radio station broadcast the Grand Ole Opry across the nation. (WSM Archives)

In the earliest days of radio, the rooms had been as dead as they could be, then in the thirties and forties they wanted them live, and in the fifties, back to dead. You know, the other day I heard one of the younger guys saying, "Man, some of that early stuff sounded good, so maybe we should go back to live." There's not really anything new, it just keeps going around and around again.

The Ryman, for example, had great acoustics, but they were uncontrollable. For certain things the big echoing sounds were great. And at that time, if you didn't have some echo, you weren't with it; if it didn't rattle around, you weren't in style.

Pioneers like Owen Bradley began to add more and more mikes and better equipment. Their experiments paid off. Soon everybody jumped on the bandwagon. I wondered where it would end.

I also began to wonder about the music *publishing* business. As I got more and more offers for my songs from New York music publishers, it made me feel that there was a definite need for a publishing house in Nashville. I went to Fred Rose to make him an offer I hoped he couldn't refuse.

My decision came right after the fourth New York publisher had offered up to twenty-five hundred dollars a song for nearly anything I could write. I had known Fred Rose for a number of years. It went back to the time he had a thirty-minute show on WSM. I had learned to respect his talent as a songwriter.

Fred had been a jazz piano player in his early days, having performed with Paul Whiteman at one time. He had cut piano rolls with Fats Waller, and had, for a time, been lured away from New York by Gene Autry, who had exhausted his supply of songs and wanted Fred to write more for him. He turned out twenty-four songs for Gene, and most of them became hits. He kept bouncing back and forth between Hollywood and New York's Tin Pan Alley, but occasionally he would stop in Nashville. Fortunately for the country music industry, he decided to stick around Nashville for a while.

I had a great deal of respect for Fred as a songwriter, so I said to him, "Fred, what we need in Nashville is a publishing house, you know that? And I'd be interested in starting one with you." He thought for a couple of minutes. "Yeah, Roy," he said, "it oughta do pretty good because there's none around." And then he changed the subject. I assumed he wasn't interested, so I sort of forgot about it. It was almost a week before I saw Fred again. He came to the Opry one night and found me backstage. "Roy," he said, "I been thinking about what you said the other day, you know, about the publishing house. Were you serious?" I told him I sure was and he said, "Well, I'd rather go into business with you than anybody I know, but I've never been able to save much money, and . . . "

I stopped him in mid-sentence. "Listen, Fred, don't you worry about the money, I'll put that up. And I'll make a deal with you: I'll supply all of the money and you supply the talent. I mean, I don't know anything about the music publishing business, so I promise you, I'll stay completely out of your way. You just run it the way you want. Besides, I'm out on the road all the time, makin' my living that way. I don't have time."

I had saved enough from the songbook sales that I could put up twenty-five thousand dollars without any problem at all. I put it in a bank account in Fred's name. Acuff-Rose Publishing Company was formed. It was the first music publishing house in the South.

Fred went to Chicago right after that and came back all encouraged. He had found somebody to do the shipping, and then he rented one room from the National Life people. It was down on Capitol Boulevard.

Fred took some of my songs and some of his and immediately started writing more, and, you know, he never did touch that initial twenty-five thousand dollars. Two months later he

The Life and Good Times of Country Music

Fred Rose. The merger of Acuff-Rose to form the first Southern music publishing house spawned some of the greatest hits in the history of country music—from songs by Hank Williams to songs by Marty Robbins. (From the collection of Les Leverett)

came to me. "I think we need a little bigger place, Roy," he said, "and, oh, by the way, I think we can handle our own shipping now."

It didn't take long for Fred to turn Acuff-Rose into a profitable business. After that, a lot of people jumped in with publishing houses, just like they had with the recording; but a lot of them weren't successful. They didn't have Fred Rose. He not only wrote some of the great songs, but he also doctored many other people's songs. Somebody would come to him with the germ of an idea or even sometimes with a good song that needed just the slightest change, and Fred would work on it, and never even suggest that they pay him anything or even put his name on it.

Some of the songs he wrote included: "Blue Eyes Crying in the Rain," "Blues on My Mind," "Fireball Mail," "Home in San Antonio," "I Can't Go On This Way," "Reap My Harvest in Heaven," "No One Will Ever Know," "Pins and Needles in My Heart," "Afraid," "Foggy River," "It's a Sin," "Roly Poly," "Sweet Kind of Love," "Take These Chains From My Heart," "Texarkana Baby," and "Waltz of the Wind." There were dozens more. And dozens that he turned into monster hits for other people. Nobody will ever know the full extent of the role Fred Rose played in song-writing in Nashville.

He wrote some songs using the names of Floyd Jenkins and Bart Dawson, because he thought they sounded a lot more like tough "hillbilly" names than "Fred Rose." He was an amazing man. He had seven dollars in his pocket when he came to Nashville, and not too many people know it, but he had had a drinking problem. It's one of the reasons he left Tin Pan Alley. I'll always be thankful that he cured it and that he came to us in Nashville. The business wouldn't have been the same without him. Oh, you would have heard of him, because he would have been writing popular songs instead of country, but at that point in the development of country music, he made a tremendous contribution. In his way, he was partly responsible for the success of the entire country music scene.

One of the biggest hits for Acuff-Rose came sort of by accident. It also became one of the largest-selling records of all time. Pee Wee King had hired Redd Stewart as a vocalist for the Golden West Cowboys. They became good friends and drove together on the road in the luggage and instrument truck used for the group.

Opry performers were still rolling in from all parts for Saturday night, just like I had always done. Well, Pee Wee and Redd were on their way back to Nashville one Friday night, listening to Bill Monroe's "Kentucky Waltz" on the

Bob Austin (left) of Cash Box *magazine presents an award to Pee Wee King for his contribution to country music. (WSM photo by Les Leverett)*

truck radio. "You know," Redd said, "It's odd that we make our living in Tennessee, and nobody's ever written a *Tennessee* waltz, at least that we know of." Pee Wee agreed. "Let's take 'The No-Name Waltz,' that old melody we been using for our theme song," Pee Wee said, "and see what we can do with some words for it." So they started writing the lyrics on the back of a matchbox. If Redd hadn't smoked cigars, we might never have had the "Tennessee Waltz."

They used the dome light on the luggage truck, and Redd wrote down the words. They changed them back and forth several times, but by the time they got to Nashville, they were pretty satisfied with what they had. They went straight to Fred Rose. Fred looked at the song and made only one change. The last phrase which finally went *I remember the night, and the Tennessee Waltz,* originally had gone, *Oh, the Tennessee Waltz, the Tennessee Waltz,* just before *Now I know how much I have lost.*

It was generally agreed that "The Tennessee Waltz" was not only the biggest hit in country music, but the biggest in popular music as well. It was the top song ever licensed by BMI (Broadcast Music Incorporated).

"The Tennessee Waltz" was typical of the type of music that country people wrote. It was simple, straight from the heart, and had a touch of sadness. There was usually sadness connected with country songs, because so many people grew up in surroundings where there wasn't a whole lot of happiness. What the depression didn't do to beat down their spirits, the drab life on a farm completed. Most farm life is hard work with little time—or even opportunity, for that matter— to have any fun at all.

And poor people seem to dwell on the hardships of life. It's why so many country songs about poverty and death and cheating wives became popular. I knew all this, and it was in the back of my mind with every song I wrote. Mine often had a religious air to them, but that was partly because the people who would be listening to them were not only poor, but also God-fearing. I was, too, so it made it easy for me.

And the songs were simple because the people were simple. They were mashed potato and chicken-fried steak simple; beer and bowling simple. There wasn't any room for a Cole Porter in country music song-writing. There isn't today.

I always tried to put as much of myself into every song I wrote as I possibly could. I figured that I was one of them and if it felt good when I wrote it, they would accept it when they heard it. And it was a whole lot more than just being commercial—trying to sell records—it was from the heart. Anything less wouldn't have come across for me, either as a songwriter or as a singer. Most of the successful songwriters did the same thing. Their songs either were a part of their own lives or showed enough of the life around them that they made sense. They were real. They might not have had the proper grammar, or even the right meter maybe, but they struck a responsive note in the people who listened to them. I guess it's why country music is so close to folk music. It's from the heart and it tells the stories of the people and the places of our time.

Most country music is traditional—blues, gospel, mountain, family kind of music. And a lot of it's about the South, particularly the hills. It started to tell of the changes, like when industry started to move down South. At times it was in anger and at other times in jest. That's when it all started to get a little more complicated. When it was just about trains and prisons and Mama and a cheatin' wife, it was more traditional than when it started to tell a story. But I saw the change coming in the sixties. Fortunately there were a few left to write the simple kind of music. I was glad that I was one of them.

Woody Guthrie was a good example of the change. He started out writing simple songs about the Southwest and it was only after he had gotten some national attention and moved to New York that his songs swung over to the folk songs with a message. As much of a country musician as he started out to be, he ended up being considered somewhat of an outsider by many Nashville musicians. His became the sophisticated music of the intellectuals.

We were lucky that people like Hank Williams and Fred Rose and Boudleaux Bryant wrote so many songs that became standards. It is always comforting, no matter what particular craze you're going through, to have songs like theirs to fall back on. We weathered the storms of folk and rockabilly and, lord knows, a lot more over the years, just by playing these standards. And when it came to writing new songs, I always used some of these standards as a sort of framework to go by.

Of course there were times when songs just popped into my head. I wrote "Precious Jewel" while we were on our way to a schoolhouse appearance. The words just came to me and I told them to Rachel, who wrote them down. It became one of my biggest hits and, according to some people, a country standard itself. It's because I *felt* it.

If I had to give somebody a lesson in songwriting, it would be a simple one: Start with an idea. You can't start with nothing. It's like trying to paint with no brush. Even if the idea just pops into your head, you've got something to start with. When two songwriters get together, they almost always have three or four ideas for a title. Chet Atkins told me how he got the idea for "How's the World Treating You?" He heard the phrase buried in a pop song, "What's New." He wrote the melody and took it to Boudleaux and said, "Here's a title and a melody, write me some lyrics."

In two hours Boudleaux wrote the words to another classic: *I've had nothing but sorrow/since you said we're through./ There's no hope for tomorrow./How's the world treating you?/ Every sweet thing that mattered/has been broken in two./All my dreams have been shattered./How's the world treating you?/Got no plans for next Sunday;/got no plans for today./ Every day is blue Monday,/every day you're away.*

Eddy Arnold took it and made a tremendous hit out of it. It's a perfect example of having something to start with. It was just like one-two-three and it was a hit song. There have been many country songs that were just that simple and they became classics. Most of them, in fact. The rest came from the public domain. They had been around for so long that a lot of times nobody even knew who wrote them. But they had been good songs and they lent themselves well to country music. Both "The Great Speckled Bird" and "Wabash Cannonball" fell into that category. I knew they would be hits for me even before I recorded them. I just didn't know they would come to be considered *my* songs, but I've gotten requests for them all over the world.

11

To hell with President Roosevelt; to hell with Babe Ruth, to hell with Roy Acuff.

—World War II Japanese battle cry

World War II probably did more to popularize country music *worldwide* than any single event in history. In the United States, it spread country music to the big cities, because so many people from the hills had gone to metropolitan areas to work in defense plants. Juke boxes in many of the cities began to contain country music songs for the first time. Soon they were filled with them.

People from Tennessee and Kentucky and West Virginia and all the "border" states swarmed to cities like Detroit and Baltimore and Akron and Chicago. There were so many people in Akron who hailed from West Virginia that it was said that the "three Rs" they taught in West Virginia schools were reading, writing and Route 21.

The requests for country music on Baltimore radio stations and juke boxes outnumbered those for popular music four to one, it was reported, and juke box owners in Detroit said that many of their coin-operated machines featured country music exclusively. The spillover effect was tremendous and within a short time, the natives of those large Northern cities, too, were listening to the music of the hills—music that had

Roy Acuff's Nashville

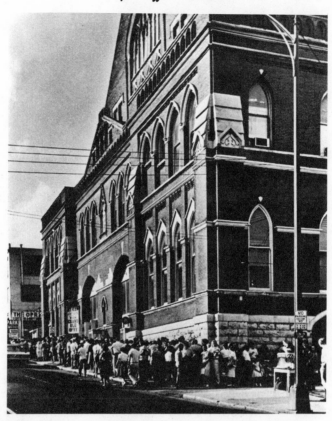

A World War II Opry crowd lines up before a Saturday night performance. Because of gasoline rationing and tire shortages, the crowds were smaller than before or after the war, but the radio audience was even larger because people were staying home more and listening to their radios. (WSM Archives)

once been limited to only the hills. The West Coast reaction was much the same, as people from the entire Southwest, particularly Oklahoma, flocked to California for defense work.

In addition to defense workers, soldiers and sailors from the South and from the hill country were stationed literally all over the world, so they had a big hand in popularizing country music, too. I was pleased to learn that our music had gotten so popular in Europe. A poll of soldiers' favorite vocalists had me in front of Frank Sinatra.

And there were country music bands springing up at military installations throughout the world. Boys who had played guitar and fiddle before they went into the service banded together to entertain their buddies. Country music was everywhere. And, in an effort to try to satisfy the appetite of servicemen for country music, the R. J. Reynolds Tobacco Company asked the Grand Ole Opry to supply a country music segment for their Camel Caravan. The Opry gave them twenty performers, including Pee Wee King and his Golden West Cowboys, Minnie Pearl, and Eddy Arnold. The group traveled more than fifty thousand miles a year and visited more than sixty Army and Navy bases, airfields, and hospitals annually, putting on more than 175 shows.

We all were doing our share of camp visits, working in as many as we could while still doing Opry performances and personal appearances to keep up the spirits of "the folks at home." It was a difficult time, but it was also a time when the nation's spirit was high and patriotism was at its ultimate level.

The biggest problem we had was in getting gasoline and tires. We wore the tread down as far as we could, had them recapped, wore them down again and went through the same thing time and time again. Finally the tires got so weak they would blow out on nearly every trip. Pee Wee King reported that he blew out thirteen tires on one trip between Kentucky and Nashville. And Minnie Pearl, who was traveling with him, says that on the last one he jumped out of the car and threatened to throw a tire iron through the windshield. It was a tough time to try to travel. The speed limit was forty miles per hour, which wasn't all that bad for most of the roads, but it slowed you down on some of them.

Minnie also told the story of one of their trips where they had been delayed so many times with tire failure that they wound up on a lonely mountain road in Pennsylvania late at night. Becky Barfield, who worked with the show, had to go to the ladies' room. The only problem was that there wasn't a

room of *any* kind, and Pee Wee had looked for a filling station
for a couple of hours. Finally, in desperation, Becky pleaded
with him to just stop anywhere. Pee Wee pulled over. It was
pitch dark outside. Becky got out the passenger side door and
disappeared. They all assumed she had gone around to the
back of the car, so they waited. And they waited. Five minutes
went by and no Becky, so Pee Wee sent one of the boys after
her. When he got around to the other side of the car, where
Becky had gotten out, he saw what had happened. The rear
wheels were parked on the very edge of a twenty-foot drop off
the mountainside, and Becky had stepped right out into thin
air. They hauled her up, brushed her off and took off down
the road. Then Becky realized that she had been so scared
she had forgotten to go.

We had to cut down the number of cars we used, because
of the tire and gasoline shortage, so we got a small trailer to
haul the instruments and luggage. This way we could load
more people in the car. Well, one night Jimmy Riddle had
crawled back into the trailer so he could sleep better. We, too,
were on a mountain road and it was a dark night. The trailer
broke loose and, as it whizzed past the car, we all watched in
horror as it rolled over a bank and down a long hill, crashing
into a tree. We screeched to a stop and tumbled down the hill
and, as we got to the trailer, Jimmy was just pulling himself
from the wreckage. He shook his head and said, "Damn, is
anybody hurt, Roy?"

It is this spirit and this humor that stand out as highlights
of the war years.

And the same spirit was reflected in the songs being
written. Red Foley had a song called "Smoke on the Water"
that told of what was going to happen when we overtook the
enemy, and Gene Autry and Tex Ritter had hits with "Have I
Stayed Away Too Long?" Gene followed with a hit that told of
the yearnings of the people back home ("I'll Wait For You,
Soldier") and another about the soldier's concerns ("At Mail
Call Today"). Tex Ritter's "Gold Star in the Window" told of

the price many paid, as did Ernest Tubb's "The Soldier's Last Letter" and the hit that I wrote and recorded, "Searching for a Soldier's Grave." There were many songs that told of our anger, like my hit "Cowards Over Pearl Harbor," and those that pointed to our pride, like Bob Wills's two hits, "Stars and Stripes on Iwo Jima" and "White Cross on Okinawa."

And there was Johnny Bond's "Draftee Blues," Cliff Bruner's "Draft Board Blues," and the Sons of the Pioneers' "They Drew My Number." There were hundreds of patriotic songs, but the king of all war songs was Elton Britt's hit "There's a Star-Spangled Banner Waving Somewhere." It told of a crippled mountain boy trying in his own way to help the war effort, pleading with his draft board to let him show what he could do to help old Uncle Sam in the war effort against the Axis powers. It was the first country song to be awarded a gold record. There had been others that sold more than a million, but it was the first to actually receive the symbolic platter. It was to be followed by many more in the country music field.

A lot of performers were doing as many *free* shows as they were paid ones—me and my boys included—and there were a lot who weren't making all that much money. But everybody was much friendlier in those days. When we all got back to the Opry on Saturday night, we would ask each other how we had done during the week. You heard every week, "Did you make enough money this week? Now, if you didn't, I did pretty well, and I can let you have some money."

Everybody enjoyed what they were doing. They went out and did a show, and they just flat enjoyed it, no matter how much or how little money they were making. It's not that way today, I'll tell you. Now there's too much money; so much, in fact, that almost nobody seems to be happy. Stars do their thing today at the Opry and leave the stage, but in those days, they used to stay around and listen to everybody else.

We put on war bond shows everywhere, which took every form you can imagine. One day Clyde Moody and Whitey

Ford, known as the Duke of Paducah, and I got a flatbed truck and parked it right in front of the old WSM studio and spent the entire Saturday putting on a live show. Anybody who bought a twenty-five-dollar war bond—which cost $18.75—could get a song dedicated to them or to anybody they selected. We sold a lot of war bonds that day.

Recording was cut back during the late stages of the war because of a vinyl shortage, so a lot of people couldn't record at all. Art Satherley cut Columbia's country music recording back to Gene Autry, Bob Wills, and me. Other companies had similar cutbacks. So again radio saved the day. I had taken over the *Prince Albert Show* on the Opry, which was the network portion. It went out to stations all over the United States on the Blue Network of the National Broadcasting System, and that did a lot to spread not only my popularity, but also that of the entire Opry. It seemed that everywhere we turned in those days, there was something good happening for country music.

We were the first country group ever to play the Venice Pier in California and we broke all attendance records for any kind of group by playing to more than seventeen thousand people there. At the Coliseum in Houston we played to eighteen thousand. We turned away so many people that I made arrangements right on the spot to rent the auditorium for two nights the following week. We played to more than seventeen thousand each of those nights, too.

I guess I was a pioneer in many areas, but I was always *prepared,* and I worked not only at being ready but also at being the best, so I was usually a step or two ahead of most of the others. I guess that's what prompted Dizzy Dean to give me the title "The King of the Hillbillies," but pretty soon newspapers and magazines included *all* of country music in the title, and it stuck.

We were the first group from the Opry to play in Florida, and they came out of the piny woods in big old cattle trucks filled with people. David Stone at WSM looked at the receipts when we got back. "Well," he said, "you drew so many people down there that we better not send you back for a year or so. I mean, we don't want to kill you off down there." But he left WSM soon after that and when Ford Rush came in to take his place, he looked at the same receipts and sent us back, and we did the same thing. We got so big, in fact, that Ford left the Artist's Service Bureau and just handled my booking. Over the years we had some high-powered agents, like Ford and Uncle Ollie Hamilton and J. L. Frank and Oscar Davis. And it paid off as we packed places like the Keil Auditorium in St. Louis and the Mosque in Richmond. We played thirty-nine fairs in one year—all the way from Louisiana to Nebraska. I remember playing in Kansas once when the sun was so hot it melted the glue on my fiddle.

It didn't seem possible, but in the forties, I was making more than two hundred thousand dollars a year.

Over the years, there have been many stories about my once leaving the Opry in anger. Well, it's true, I did leave the Opry. I left for a year, but I left with the blessing of everybody on the show. There was no dispute over salary with the Opry people or any truth to the rumors of hard feelings between Ernest Tubb and me. Ernest and I have never had any words or even a disagreement. I left the Opry because I wanted to go to the West Coast. And for a very good reason. On the Opry, I was making five hundred dollars a week. On the West Coast I could make twenty-five hundred dollars a week. So the reason was pure and simple. Actually there were two thousand reasons. And all of them dollars. I took my boys, who now included Howard (Howdy) Forrester, and headed West.

When I left the Opry, they brought in Red Foley to take my place as the headliner. And it was a good choice. He had come from much the same background as the rest of us. The story goes that Red grew up singing in the blackberry patches around his home in Berea, Kentucky. He and his classmates in a one-room school were threatened with a hickory stick if they didn't sing at the top of their lungs, so that's how he learned to sing loud.

Red's father was a storekeeper and he took in an old guitar on a grocery bill. Well, Red took it over and learned to play it, using his thumb instead of a pick. A WLS talent scout found Red some time later and offered him a job on the Chicago radio station. He starred with Lulu Belle (who later teamed up with Scotty to form one of the best duos in country music) and they made some records for the Conqueror label. Later they went into partnership to form the Renfro Valley Barn Dance, but Red only stayed there for three years. He went back to WLS, where he worked in the Chuck Wagon Gang and the Brown's Ferry Four. He also got a record contract with Decca and later a network show with Red Skelton.

Another singer came to Nashville about this time: Eddy Arnold, "The Tennessee Plowboy." Eddy told me one time, "I was about fifteen when I decided to start trying show business. I had been messing around with the guitar since I was about nine or ten, so I started to perform at parties and I really got the bug. Then one day I got to be on *radio* with my school. That did it. I talked them into letting me work on the station, and they did.

"They didn't pay me anything," Eddy said, "because I wasn't worth anything. But I got experience and went on to get a better job with a Memphis radio station."

Also during this period, Eddy worked in a funeral home, where he did everything: drove the ambulance, put water in the pitcher, and was a "general flunky." But he got a free room and board. It took him a few years and a few more jobs before he landed a recording contract, but when he did, things happened pretty fast for him. A little over a year after he recorded "Mommy, Please Stay Home with Me," he cut "That's How Much I Love You," and it sold 650,000 records. He was on his way.

Eddy did a lot to change people's image of country music. With his fine voice, he swayed a lot of people from pop to country music. In fact, many people called him "the Frank Sinatra of *pop* country music." But in Nashville, they were more inclined to call Frank Sinatra "the Eddy Arnold of the pop field."

Eddy may have started a trend toward the soft, smooth style of singing, because a succession of such stars soon emerged. Artists like George Morgan, Eddie Kirk, Wesley Tuttle, Wally Fowler, Zeke Clements, and Leon Payne had pretty much the same style. And country began to blend more and more with pop music. Ernest teamed up with the Andrew Sisters on "Don't Rob Another Man's Castle." Jimmy Wakely and Margaret Whiting had big hits with "One Has My Name, the Other Has My Heart" and "Slipping Around"; and Tennessee Ernie Ford and Kay Starr pleased both pop and country fans with "Nobody's Business" and "I'll Never Be Free."

Country music entered the fifties not just as an accepted form of American music, but as a very popular one.

12

Did you ever see a robin weep
when leaves begin to die
That means he's lost the will to live
I'm so lonesome I could cry.

—*Hank Williams*

I had been in touch with the Opry all along, and had even done *Prince Albert* network portions from California. But they asked me to come back because the show in Nashville wasn't going as well as it had before. So I returned.

The Grand Ole Opry had passed WLS's *National Barn Dance* by the late forties, but another station had also started to challenge the WLS supremacy. KWKH in Shreveport was having great success with the *Louisiana Hayride.* They produced such stars as Webb Pierce, Slim Whitman, Jim Reeves, Kitty Wells, and Johnny, Jack, and Faron Young, and for a while it looked as if they might even take the top spot. But despite the outstanding talent they had, the Opry still reigned supreme. The way you could tell it was this: The minute a star got big on the *Hayride,* he or she jumped right to the Opry. So the *Hayride* became known as the "Cradle of the Stars," a sort of minor-league farm system for the Opry.

That's certainly not to say that it wasn't an important show. It was. Because the stars that came from Shreveport were not

Webb Pierce's early performances momentarily shifted country music's emphasis from Nashville to the Southwest. (WSM photo by Les Leverett)

only true stars, they were also well-trained and Opry-ready by the time they got to Nashville.

Webb Pierce is a good example. His voice was high and he always sang right at the top of his range, but it was such a different style that he was an immediate success. He had twenty-one records that hit the number-one spot in the fifties, including "Back Street Affair," "Wondering," "More and More," "I'm in the Jailhouse Now," and his honky-tonk masterpiece, "There Stands the Glass."

To get experience, he had first appeared on the *Hayride* for free. He had a job at Sears and Roebuck, selling shoes, and he "really didn't need the money," he said. "I just want to be in show business." He got there with a series of quick hit records.

Faron Young came along at the same time. He sounded like most other country singers at first, but little by little he began to develop a mellow style, sort of like crooning. His hit "Five Dollars and a Saturday Night" brought him to the whole country's attention.

Another great singer, Ray Price, had enough of a different style to attract attention. He combined Western and country styles, and his fine voice was always accompanied by a big sound—three or four fiddles and a heavy beat.

And Hank Thompson had a big, rich sound. He always reminded me of Mel Tillis, but his hit "Wild Side of Life" may have started a trend. When he sang that first line about not knowing God made honky-tonk angels, it became his trademark. It was one of the first country songs, or at least one of the first to become a national hit, that told about getting drunk and raising hell. With the success of that first song, Kitty Wells countered with the woman's viewpoint on her monster hit, "It Wasn't God Who Made Honky-Tonk Angels."

Kitty was as pure a "country" singer the business had ever produced and it was not only predictable but also proper that she was to become the "Queen of Country Music." And Kitty held that title for probably fifteen years before she semi-retired and Loretta Lynn took it over.

Big bands backed at least two singers of the era. Carl Smith, who came from my hometown of Maynardville, and Little Jimmy Dickens really turned people on with their approach to country music. It was a period when artists were reaching out and trying everything to gain attention. And record sales reflected it.

But there was one performer whose star shone brighter then, and probably always will: Hank Williams. He was

Faron Young. (WSM photo by Les Leverett)

Stoney Cooper (left) and Ray Price at the Opry. Price's mellow voice brought him acclaim from pop music critics as well. (WSM photo by Les Leverett)

Kitty Wells. (WSM photo by Les Leverett)

working in Shreveport when I first met him. He and his wife, Audrey, came to all of my shows every time I was in the area, and they came backstage after the show and talked for as long as we had time. If we were staying over, we usually went out to some honkytonk where Hank was playing and my boys and I would sit in with Hank. It wasn't the sort of atmosphere I really liked, but I could see what a tremendous talent he was, and I enjoyed listening to him. Besides, he wanted to study my style and how I handled myself on the stage and that was flattering to me.

One night he sat in my dressing room and sang a song he had written. He sat there—or rather "hunkered" there—and played and sang "I Saw the Light," and I was really impressed. I asked him if he wanted to record it, and he said he did. I contacted Fred Rose and told him I had a boy I wanted him to work with. The world knows the rest. Hank was an original.

He once said he wrote songs "because they just come bustin' out. I never wrote a note, except in my heart." All that was true. His mother said, "In all my life I never knew my son to just sit down to write a song. Like he said, 'they just come bustin' out.' If people liked his songs, he was glad—but he would have written them anyway, because he felt them so much he had to sing them."

Hank was born in a log cabin in 1923 in Mount Olive, Alabama, to a poor family. When he was about five, he went to work shining shoes and selling peanuts, and on his first day of work he made thirty cents. His mother told me that he brought home stew meat, tomatoes, and rice and asked her to make gumbo stew.

But, according to Hank, it took an old Negro street singer named "Tee Tot" to really get him fired up to music. Tee Tot sang the blues like only the old Negro street singers could, and I guess that memory of those mournful songs and the beat-up old guitar never left Hank. At least, he never stopped talking about it. It also influenced almost everything he ever

Hank Williams. (WSM Archives)

wrote—the earthy language of his Southern heritage and the troubles of the working people.

His mother added the final ingredient when she bought Hank a second-hand guitar for $3.50. At the time she was making twenty-five cents a day by nursing and sewing. When the family moved to Montgomery, Hank was twelve years old, and he entered a talent show. He sang his first original composition, "WPA Blues," and he won the fifteen-dollar prize, which was a lot of money in 1935. It was money won during the depression by singing *about* the depression.

And Hank was an immediate show business success, because most of the people in the theater that night knew all too well about the WPA, and the song hit so close to their own lives that they stomped and applauded. His formula for "down-to-earth" songs had worked in his first attempt—at twelve years of age.

He was still selling peanuts and shining shoes when he started singing in clubs and honkytonks. And he was still only twelve. It's little wonder that his life turned out so tragically, because I don't think there was anybody who had such a hard time from the start. He told me about having to ruin some guitars by breaking them over people's heads in fights that broke out in the clubs.

Hank formed his own band when he was thirteen, "The Drifting Cowboys," and adopted the name "Luke the Drifter" for himself. He performed on WSFA radio in Montgomery and played honkytonks at night. Being up half the night, he usually slept through school, and I guess it explains why he had so little formal education. Hank was almost illiterate and he butchered the King's English worse, I guess, than anybody I ever heard. But when he picked up a stubby pencil and had a song in his heart he was as much of a poet as anybody who ever lived. He was brilliant.

When Hank came to Nashville to meet Fred Rose, he was as nervous as a cat. He never did have much confidence in himself, despite the enormous talent he had. But Fred could tell immediately what a tremendous talent he had, and they quickly became the greatest team Nashville ever saw. Fred signed him immediately for Acuff-Rose and got him a recording contract with MGM.

It was Audrey—or, at least, the love affair they had—that inspired Hank to write many of his great ballads. I think it was mainly because they loved each other like the lovers in the old ballads. Out of their joys and troubles and spats came dozens of ballads like, "They'll Never Take Her Love From Me," "Why Don't You Love Me Like You Used To Do?" "Cold, Cold Heart," and "You Win Again." The words to "You Win Again" told a lot of how he felt: *The news is all over town/that you've been seen runnin' around. /I know I should leave, but then/I just can't go. You win again.*

Hank was on his way. He got a job on the *Louisiana Hayride* and just bided his time until the call came from the Opry. In the meantime, he and Fred kept cranking out Hank's hit songs. Fred sat at that little white piano of his and polished the songs into great hits. I really liked Hank and I was pleased with his success, but a lot of people sort of put some of the songs down. "Too slick," they said. You know, a lot of people think that if it doesn't smell like tanbark all over it's no good. But Hank had something different. I mean who but an absolute poet would write words like: *Did you ever see a robin weep/when leaves begin to die/That means he's lost the will to live/I'm so lonesome I could cry,* or *I've never seen a night so long/when time goes crawling by./ The moon just went behind a cloud/to hide its face and cry.*

Hank's Opry call came in 1949. There were rumors that he drank too much and raised hell and that he was hard to work with. They were mostly true, but the Opry could no longer ignore the impact he was having on music—*all* music.

Hank showed up in Nashville in June of 1949 for his first Opry appearance and, as usual, he was unsure of himself. Most people never saw this because he covered it up with a sort of arrogant, cocky attitude. As he stood out in front of the

Roy Acuff's Nashville

Ryman Auditorium, looking up at that big, cold-looking building, I'd be willing to bet that he was scared half to death. But a kid walked up to him and said, "Hey, mister, you on the Opry?" "I might be, son. Who's your favorite singer?" he asked. "Little Jimmy Dickens," the boy replied. "Well," Hank said, "you just keep a eye out for Hank Williams, you hear?" And he walked down the street to Tootsie's Orchid Lounge and looked in. Tootsie's was where a lot of the Opry regulars hung out and Hank knew he would be in there that night, drinking beer with the rest.

There were more than thirty-five hundred people in the audience as Hank stood backstage. I looked around to make sure he was there. Everybody was quiet during the introduction. "Ladies and gentlemen, there isn't a music fan anywhere that hasn't heard this next man and thrilled to this songs. It's his first Opry appearance so let's make this great star welcome. Here he is ladies and gentlemen, straight from the fields of Alabama, Hank Williams."

Hank strolled out on the stage. He was tall and lanky and he had on a tan cowboy suit and tan cowboy hat. He rocked back and forth a couple of times on the heels of his cowboy boots, then he sort of slumped over the microphone and started tapping his foot. He went right into "Lovesick Blues." He had made a good record of the song, but what happened at this performance, nobody expected. He got a standing ovation and ended up doing six encores. The applause lasted for five minutes after he went back into his dressing room.

For the next three years, Hank played the Opry—when he wasn't drunk—just to build up the demand for himself on the road show circuit. He wasn't making that much money on the Opry, but in one year, his fees went from $250 a night to over $1,000, which was top dollar for a performer in those days.

Fred took a handful of his songs to New York, because he was convinced that they could make just as big a hit in the pop field as they would in country. Mitch Miller, who was then head of recording at Columbia, bought "Cold, Cold Heart" for one of his new singers, a kid named Tony Bennett. The record that came from that combination became number one and launched Tony Bennett on his phenomenal career. It also completely broke down the barrier that had stood between country and pop music. It was surely one of the most important things that ever happened to American music.

Nobody had ever seen a star like Hank before. He had some sort of magic sex appeal to the women in the audience and when he swayed his hips and gyrated—like Elvis Presley was to do later—they went wild. And the men didn't seem to feel threatened by it. He just had this magnetism to his stage presence.

But it wasn't always there when he was *off*stage. At times he was downright belligerent. I guess he might have had a chip on his shoulder because so many people had ignored him on the way up.

For example, long before he became a star, he had come to the Opry one time for an audition. Jud Collins held the audition and told Hank, "I'll call you if I ever need you." Well, Hank never forgot that dismissal. (That's what he considered it.) After he had become a star he went up to Jud one night at the Opry and said, "Hey, Jud, you remember that day when I gave you my name and address and you were going to get in touch with me if you ever needed me?"

"Yeah, I sure made a mistake, didn't I?" Jud laughed.

"Well, I got three Cadillacs. How many you got?" Hank said, as he walked away.

But underneath Hank was still insecure. As beautiful as most of his lyrics were, he never thought anybody else would think so. "You think people will get that, Roy?" he would ask. I always told him they would because I *knew* they would, but he would walk away, shaking his head, saying, "Damn, I'm not sure, Roy. I'm not sure."

Or he would conduct his own personal poll. He would stop some of the top artists in the hall and say, "Hey, hoss, listen to this song I just wrote. I might let you have it." And he would stand there with his face about an inch or two away, about knocking you over with his bourbon breath, and he would sing every verse of it. If he got enough favorable response from people like Ernest Tubb or Hank Snow, he would say, "Well, to hell with you, I'm going to record it myself. Hell, it's too good for you." It was his own personal Gallup poll. But it didn't make him all that popular with a lot of other artists.

And he didn't always treat his fans with a whole lot of love. One night, for instance, as he left the Opry, a man came up and slapped him on the back. The man had a lot of friends with him, undoubtedly all fans of Hank. "How ya doin', Hank?" he asked. "How'm I doin'? Well, I'm not doin' too bad for a boy who used to shine shoes and sell peanuts on the street. Ain't that right, *friend?*" He pronounced the word "friend" in a way that had no friendliness in it at all. The man's face turned red and he left. And Hank left.

Fred Rose always stuck by him, and he became a sort of father image to Hank. Fred dressed up Hank's songs, looked after his personal appearances and his recordings by getting the proper side men for his sessions and making sure the musical arrangements were right for Hank. He loaned Hank money in the early days and tried to save Hank's marriage in the later ones. No song was ever recorded without Fred's approval, and no recording session was ever held unless Fred or his son, Wesley, who he had brought in to help run Acuff-Rose, was present.

But Hank's life began to fall apart. His drinking was wearing him down and, if that wasn't enough, pills were finishing him off. His health broke under the strain of his work, and when his marriage failed completely, Hank came apart. A lot of people thought that the way Hank suffered over a song was all part of the act, but his friends knew that the suffering was real. He suffered every minute.

He got so drunk up in Canada one time that he fell off the stage. They had to get the Mounties to get the group out of town because the crowd was so angry.

The Opry finally had to fire him in August of 1952 because of his drinking. Audrey had divorced him, and Hank was a broken man. Only Hank knew why he did it. It's not my place to judge him, but I know he was driven to it. It was just one thing right after another. I know there are still a lot of people who wish they could have made the mark Hank did. His songs are like the songs of Stephen Foster; they'll be around forever.

Hank thought he was left with only his mother, who loved him dearly. But she was about as tough as Hank, and she did stick by him. He once told me the most incredible story about her I ever heard. He said he used to get in a lot of honkytonk brawls in the days when he was playing those places as a kid. And one night a guy beat him up so bad that he was left for dead in the parking lot. A cab driver pulled into the lot and saw Hank lying in a pool of blood, and he recognized him, so he took him home to his mother. She looked at Hank and said, "First we get you sewed up; then we go get him." Then he told me, "There ain't nobody in the whole world I'd rather have alongside me in a fight than my mama with a broken beer bottle in her hand."

When the end came, he felt he had nobody else. He thought the world had deserted him, but he was really wrong. There were still some who loved him. He just didn't see it, except maybe in two others. The ones whose love he did see, other than his mother, were his children, Hank, Jr., and Lycrecia, particularly Hank, Jr., whom he called "Bosephus . . ." In fact, one of his best-known phrases was one that he closed many of his performances with: "If the good Lord's willin' and the creeks don't rise, I'll be with you again, Bosephus."

On New Year's Eve, 1952, his sister, Irene, who was a self-proclaimed mystic, awoke from a deep sleep. She grasped her throat and screamed, "Hank just died!"

A few hours later, his chauffeur—driving through the hills of West Virginia with Hank asleep in the back seat, full of drugs and booze—decided to stop the Cadillac limousine and check on his boss. He hadn't heard anything from him for a long time. But Luke the Drifter had already drifted into "Hillbilly Heaven."

13

*The Nashville Sound began to take over
where rockabilly had left off.*

The theme for a lot of country music in the fifties had become drinking and running around, but there was something happening that was bringing back a lot of the original themes and sounds. Bill Monroe was again making traditional music popular with what he called "bluegrass music."

Actually bluegrass was not that much different from what we had been playing all along. And a lot of times the only difference was in who was playing it. I mean, if I played a certain song it was considered "country," but if Bill Monroe played the same song, it was considered "bluegrass."

But there *was* a difference, and I was mighty pleased to see Bill getting the recognition he deserved. His songs emphasized some of the folk themes of traditional country music, like family and sentiment and lost love, instead of hell-raising and cheating. But, more than that, they brought back the basic string group of guitar, fiddle, and banjo. The main difference was that with my music, the fiddle dominated the banjo and guitar; in bluegrass, the banjo was the lead instrument. Also, other members of Bill's band took solos, which made it a lot like jazz in that respect. They used a mandolin and a rolling, three-finger banjo-picking style that had been developed by Earl Scruggs, some years before. And Scruggs,

Roy Acuff's Nashville

Lester Flatt (left) and Earl Scruggs. Their sound became known to the whole country when they recorded the theme song for the TV series The Beverly Hillbillies. *(WSM photo by Les Leverett)*

along with Lester Flatt, became almost as popular as Bill Monroe.

As Acuff-Rose expanded, it began to attract more and more songwriters. One of these was Marty Robbins, who not only wrote good songs, but also sang them well. In fact, he was probably my favorite of the period. His hits "Time Goes By" and "At the End of a Long Lonely Day" were Opry favorites. But he made the crossover into pop and rock with the smash hits "A White Sport Coat and a Pink Carnation" and Chuck Berry's "Maybelline."

In fact, there were many country performers who were crossing the line into rock; so many, in fact, that the term "rockabilly" was being used to describe their music. The music scene shifted from Nashville to Memphis, where some extremely popular singers were recording, the leading one, of course, being Elvis Presley. But Elvis wasn't the only one.

There were Roy Orbison, Jerry Lee Lewis, Johnny Cash, and Carl Perkins, and their records were selling so well for a small record label named Sun that Nashville recording studios began to take them very seriously. What they had considered a fly-by-night label was suddenly the hottest one in the country.

There had already been many rock-type hits in country music over the years, going all the way back to the Delmore Brothers, who had recorded what was called "hillbilly boogie" in the thirties. Red Foley's "Tennessee Saturday Night" and Hank Williams's "Rootie Tootie" both could be described as "rock," but this new wave turned some one-time country stars into the absolute kings of rock.

Few people remember that Bill Haley started as a country music performer. In the late forties, he had a band called Bill Haley and the Four Aces of Western Swing. Yet he was the first major white rock singer and probably the person who took rock to the very top of the pop charts.

Sam Phillips's Sun label released its first country record in 1953—"Silver Bells" by the Ripley Cotton Choppers—and it was clearly labeled "hillbilly." But six months later, Phillips recorded Elvis singing "Blue Moon of Kentucky." The arrangement was totally different than it had been when Bill Monroe recorded the song in 1945 for Columbia, but that "different" style was to make musical history.

Elvis was nineteen years old when he recorded that song, with "That's All Right" on the B side. He signed a year later with RCA and recorded in Nashville in January of 1956 with, among other sidemen, Chet Atkins on guitar and Floyd Cramer on piano. His first recording, "Heartbreak Hotel," became a standard among rockabilly songs and was number one on both pop and country charts. Everybody knows the rest of the Elvis story, but not too many people know that Jerry Lee Lewis, not Elvis, had the two *biggest* hits for Sun records. His gigantic hits "Whole Lot of Shakin' Goin' On" and "Great Balls of Fire" were the top records *ever* for Sun,

Elvis Presley and Hank Snow. (WSM Archives)

Roy Orbison. (WSM photo by Les Leverett)

Jerry Lee Lewis. (WSM photo by Les Leverett)

and they were also chart-busters in country, pop, *and* rhythm and blues.

One of the rockabilly greats never made it to the country charts. Buddy Holly's music was maybe too "soft" for both the country fans and the hard-core rock fans. It is possible that he might have made the country charts had he not been killed in a plane crash in 1959.

But another rockabilly act did thrill country audiences and easily made it to the top of the country charts several times— the Everly Brothers. Their pop hits "Bye Bye Love," "Wake Up Little Suzie," and "All I Have To Do Is Dream" were also major rockabilly hits.

The sixties saw rockabilly beginning to fade in Nashville. What was taking its place would make Nashville one of the most—if not *the* most—important recording centers in the whole world. People started to refer to the type of records coming out of the city as "the Nashville Sound," and with all of the new recording studios and the outstanding sidemen, the Sound began to take over where rockabilly was leaving off; or, more accurately, being *pushed* out of the limelight.

I think it was the sidemen who made the real difference. These studio musicians had played together for so long, and they had developed a style so smooth and easy, that recording artists coming from New York, for example, couldn't believe it. They were not only relaxed, they were also creative and easy to work with. They knew one another's styles so well that in minutes they could work out arrangements that took other studio musicians in other cities hours, or maybe days.

The Sound began as a single group of sidemen, who moved from studio to studio, working on the recording sessions of as many singers or instrumentalists as happened to be recording in Nashville. As the number of sessions grew, the number of sidemen grew. And they were mostly talented, trained musicians who could read music if they had to, but preferred to play it by ear, since country music had always been more

Chet Atkins (left) presenting Jim Reeves with his first gold record for his hit "He'll Have to Go." (WSM photo by Les Leverett)

folksy in its approach. The message or lyrics of the song was the most important thing, so the basic musical structure was always simple. The most basic musical progression would handle many country songs, so detailed charts usually weren't needed. Since country songs usually didn't change tempo, there wasn't any need for time signatures. This kept everything so simple that the same chord changes could be repeated over and over again, and could serve as perfect accompaniment for many songs, whether for my recording of "The Great Speckled Bird" or for Ernest Tubb's "Walking the Floor Over You."

The new Nashville Sound—actually it was as old as Nashville recording, but it was "new" to a lot of outsiders—was strong on the sounds of the rhythm section, particularly the guitar. Actually, it was usually guitars, because there was normally more than one. If two acoustic guitars were used, one was often pitched high to give a ringing sound to the chord. An electric guitar usually played lead, and there were variations on how it was tuned, according to what effect was wanted. Sometimes it sounded like a standard electric guitar and sometimes it sounded more like a fiddle run. An upright string bass was used to give the sound some style.

Even the breaks—or solos, as they call them today—were simple. It was this simplicity that appealed not only to recording artists but also to record buyers all over the world. The whole thing was very similar to what we had been doing for years; that became very evident when a Dobro guitar was added to Tom T. Hall's great song, "Harper Valley PTA," which became a runaway hit for Jeannie C. Riley.

While the Nashville Sound was developing, so were two outstanding singers, Jim Reeves and Patsy Cline. Jim came from the same area of Texas that produced country music great Tex Ritter, and had turned to country music in exactly the same fashion as I had. He had a contract to play baseball with a major-league team, the St. Louis Cardinals. And his major-league plans ended just about as abruptly as mine had. He was injured in a minor-league game and could never play again. So he turned to music as a career.

He had started playing guitar when he was seven years old, on a six-string guitar for which he had traded a bushel of pears. But little Jimmy's six-string guitar had only three strings. That didn't matter to him, though. He still taught himself to play, and it later gave him something to fall back on when he had to give up baseball.

A series of radio jobs and a couple of hit records led him to the Opry in 1955. Those songs were fairly big sellers, but in 1957 his record "Four Walls" put him near the top in country and pop polls.

Patsy had come to Nashville for the first time in 1948 and I

Jeannie C. Riley. (WSM photo by Les Leverett)

had a chance to hear her first audition. She was only sixteen years old but was so good that I offered her a spot on my radio program. Her money ran out and she had to go back to Winchester, her hometown in Virginia. She had started there by singing anyplace anybody would listen to her, whether in church or on the street corner. And she used to go to the radio station in Winchester and sing for free for any country acts that came to town. That's how she met Walley Fowler, who had a group called the Oak Ridge Quartet, and who frequently appeared on my show.

It was nearly ten years after that audition when she came back to Nashville. She had gotten a big break by singing "Walking After Midnight" on Arthur Godfrey's *Talent Scouts* television show and had won first prize. She quickly became the top female singer in the country music field, but then she gave up singing for a few years to "just be a housewife." She missed singing and, by 1960, she was on the Opry and had a recording contract with Decca. Her version of "I Fall to Pieces" was one of many smash hits she recorded after that.

Patsy Cline. (WSM photo by Les Leverett)

Patsy and Jim were both superstars in the early sixties, but within one year they both were gone, tragic victims of separate private airplane crashes. The crash that took Patsy's life also robbed us of Cowboy Copas and Hawkshaw Hawkins.

It was a period that took a lot of us a long time to get over, because we lost so much great talent from the Opry. There was a while, in fact, when the Opry was said to be jinxed. But the jinx seemed to finally fade away and be forgotten, and when it was gone, country music had finally emerged again from what could have been its own ashes.

Rock and roll—or rockabilly, as they wanted to call it in Nashville—had robbed country music of some fine talent.

Elvis and Carl Perkins and Jerry Lee Lewis and the Everly Brothers and a lot of the others never really returned to the country scene, but fortunately some musicians did. Conway Twitty and Marty Robbins were two that came back and became great *country* stars.

Business was operating as usual on Nashville's Music Row and, with the decline of rock and renewed interest in country music, some new stars were coming along to crank out hit records. Columbia could boast of Tammy Wynette and George Jones and Sonny James. Nearly every studio in town was producing stars. In fact, a whole new era of stars like Connie Smith (a favorite of mine), Merle Haggard, Dolly Parton, Glen Campbell, Charlie Pride, Roger Miller, and Buck Owens came along to produce hit records. And some of the artists who had been around for some time, like Porter Wagoner and Johnny Cash, had new hits.

Even comedy began to return to country music. What had once been so important a part of almost all country music shows, but had long ago faded, found its way back. Most of the early comedians were gone—Uncle Dave and Rod Brasfield and many others had passed on—but there were still some of the funniest people around. Minnie Pearl, fortunately for all of us, had been with the Opry all along and still thrilled audiences with her warm and boisterous welcome: 'How-dee. I'm so glad to be here."

So when a summer television replacement show came on, it came to stay. And it returned much of the old feeling to the country music scene. *Hee Haw,* not only brought us some of the great comedians again, like Grandpa Jones, Archie Campbell, Stringbean, and even Minnie Pearl from time to time, but it also became a TV showcase for some of country music's best vocal and instrumental artists.

The whole style of the program was just like my old tent shows—a mixture of humor, serious songs, slapstick, hymns, and old-time and modern music.

It was a pleasure to me to see a show like *Hee Haw* make it.

Tammy Wynette. (WSM photo by Les Leverett)

It was a little like taking a step back in time. Actually, *I* never moved forward. The rest of country music did. At least, most of it. People like Ernest Tubb and Hank Snow and I stayed right at the Opry, doing the same kind of music we had always done. Because of that, I don't really know too much about the stars of the last twenty years. Maybe it's just that old-timers like to stick together, but I'd sooner think that it's because we've stayed right in our little nest, playing our own music, and ignored the changes.

At one time or another, though, all of the stars of today get to the Opry, and I'm starting to get to know them a little better. If I ever decide to retire, maybe I'll write a sequel to this book and bring everybody up to date, but for right now, I wanted to write about the people and the things and the

Grandpa Jones and I on Hee Haw. *(Roy Acuff Collection)*

music that made country music what it is today—about the
early years. My years.

One thing I am sure of, though: Things didn't happen all
that much different for some of the newer stars than they did
for the early ones. It's just that there is so much more money
around and so much more exposure because of televison and
fast transportation. But maybe that's taken a lot of the fun out
of it.

Gene Autry being inducted into the Country Music Hall of Fame in 1969.
With him are Tennessee Ernie Ford and Tex Ritter. (Nashville Area
Chamber of Commerce).

Still, performers and songwriters are teaming up to crank out new "standards." New songwriters and new stars appear on the scene every day. And in some cases, established songwriters give tunes to new stars.

Songwriters like Billy Edd Wheeler and Kris Kristofferson have turned out hits for new stars and old ones. And artists like Willie Nelson and Waylon Jennings have achieved stardom, even though they have been around for years. In fact, for every Barbara Mandrell or Lynn Anderson or Tammy Wynette or Loretta Lynn, who have virtually started out as stars, there are a dozen more like Willie and Waylon who have been around for years and then suddenly made it.

By the seventies, the section of Nashville around the Ryman Auditorium had become a little seedy. There were taverns and massage parlors and prostitutes, and it bothered the WSM management. The area around Fourth and Broadway

Loretta Lynn with Conway Twitty. (WSM photo by Les Leverett)

no longer was proper for their family show image. And the building was getting pretty dilapidated.

They planned to move. Immediately the "Save the Opry" cry went up. Everybody expected me to sort of lead the drive, because I was one of the only regulars who had been there when they moved into the Ryman. I shocked a lot of people when I took the stand that the Opry *should* move to the new Opryland, a few miles outside of Nashville. Oh, I hated to think about leaving the old building. It was the home that had done the most for the image of the Opry. But, I'll tell you, I

Waylon Jennings. Like Willie Nelson, Waylon was beardless during his Nashville career until stardom struck. (WSM photo by Les Leverett)

worried every Saturday night when I looked up into that balcony and saw it packed. That old building was going to fall in someday, I felt it, and it would have been the worst tragedy I could think of. In addition to my concerns about the safety of the building, I knew we needed better facilities. The dressing-room space had been inadequate for years and everything, generally, was just outdated for the kind of show we were putting on.

So I was one of the happiest people in Nashville when, in 1974, we moved to the new Opry. Os and Howdy and Jimmy Riddle and Charlie Collins had been with me a long time, and they were happy, too. For one thing, it is the most advanced and modern auditorium in the world. We have nice, bright dressing rooms, and the sound system and the acoustics are the best anywhere. If you've never been there, you owe it to yourself just to see it. It is an outstanding facility, and a perfect spot for the next fifty years of the Grand Ole Opry.

The Grand Ole Opry House, new home of the Grand Ole Opry. (Nashville Area Chamber of Commerce)

Still I was sad when we left the Ryman. I stood there on the stage after everything had been moved out and I just thought of the years of joy and laughter and truly fine music that had poured out over that stage. I could just see Uncle Dave twirling his banjo over his head and I could hear Hank Williams singing. And for some reason, I thought of Minnie Pearl and Rod Brasfield, and of one of their comedy routines. Rod's false teeth didn't fit right, and he used them beautifully by clacking them at the proper time of a joke. "By Ned, buddy," was his favorite saying. The routine I thought of went like this:

Rod: "By Ned, buddy. Miss Minnie, I sure do wanna walk you home tonight (and he clacked his teeth). I always wanted to walk home with an experienced girl."

Minnie: "But, Rod, I'm not experienced."

Rod: "Yes, and you ain't home yet neither (*clack, clack*)."

The Life and Good Times of Country Music

Here I am giving President Nixon a yo-yo Lesson, during opening ceremonies on the new Opry. (WSM photo by Les Leverett)

Epilogue

"Roy Acuff, the Smoky Mountain Boy,
fiddled and sang his way into the hearts of
millions the world over, often times bringing country
music to areas where it had never
been heard before . . ."

—Hall of Fame plaque

I'm constantly asked to pick a high point in my life. That's not easy, because there are so many wonderful things that have happened to me. Certainly my life with Mildred was the personal highlight; and the birth of our son, Roy Neill. But as far as my *career* is concerned, there are many: coming to the Opry as a regular, then doing the *Prince Albert* network portion of the show; playing the Palace Theater in New York, and Carnegie Hall and Madison Square Garden; introducing President Nixon when he dedicated the new Opry, riding in Air Force One with John Wayne to entertain POWs at the White House. All of these were high points. Having not one but two stars in the Walk of Stars in Hollywood and having my footprints in front of the Chinese Theater there are important to me.

Fifty years in show business itself is a high point; I mean, just to think that I got paid all of those years for doing something I love so much is unbelievable. I think I would have done it for nothing if I hadn't gotten paid. The money was always secondary. There were a lot of performers in the early days who felt that way. It's all changed now. A lot of them swap off the name *country* for money. Why they don't want to keep a country image, I don't know. They call it country *rock* or country *pop*, anything but pure old *country*. *Hillbilly* is still good enough for me. I'm proud of it, because it makes me different from most other people.

But then the whole scene is different today. When I started, one good band could make a living doing road shows. Today they have to have package tours, where you have maybe half a dozen names on a bill, and they have to get up to fifteen dollars a ticket. But it's the only way they can get a full house and show a profit. I had to *make a living* in the early days out of country music, playing every night, not just weekends. And even then, that's why a lot of them didn't make it. They didn't have the commitment it took. They couldn't hold on long enough to make it.

Oh, as the Opry began to get bigger and road shows started to pick up, a lot of people could see some brightness in it, but back when I first started it was all dark. There was no brightness at all. I had no thought of ever making a *living* out of music. I mean, a real living. I was doing it for fun.

There are a few artists around today who would have made it back then. I think Marty Robbins would have. He's a great artist, and he'll tell it like it is. But most of the others seem to lack sparkle. And a lot of the rest just don't want to stay with country music. I think Barbara Mandrell is trying to stay with it. And certainly Loretta Lynn is; she's a lovely person to be around. But Dolly Parton has drifted farther away than most of them. She's become a Hollywood glamour girl, and that's a shame for us because she used to write some good songs.

A lot of them have drifted away over the years. Take Johnny Cash, for example. If he had stayed with the Opry, he would have been one of the Opry greats, but he wanted to be another John Wayne. He did make a big comeback, though,

With Dolly Parton. (WSM photo by Les Leverett)

Johnny Cash, whose music has appealed to both country and rock fans. (WSM photo by Les Leverett)

which I think he owes a lot to his wife, June. I'm proud of him. He overcame some big problems and he's a star again.

Some of them didn't overcome the problems—like Elvis. There wasn't a nicer boy in the world when he first came to Nashville. He had an electricity about him, whether he was on the stage or off. But his manager, Colonel Tom Parker, just exposed him almost to death. He would put Elvis where the crowd already was (he had done the same thing with Eddy Arnold); I mean, places like the Fat Stock Show in Houston, or *any*place where there were thousands of people. He would give out free tickets to high-school girls to come down and scream. It finally hurt Elvis, because he got to the point where he was afraid to come out of his hotel. Instead of being outside with all his friends, he was up in some hotel room, living like a hermit. It's no wonder he turned to drugs. It's like chaining a dog to a stake. You have to have your freedom.

A lot of performers have always had bodyguards, but I've never felt the need for one. I've never felt crowded in show business. Oh, a few times people have rubbed me the wrong way, but I've handled it myself.

You can go bad right quick in the entertainment business. And I don't like to see it. It hurts me to see some of the artists drunk or stoned all the time. I think it belittles all of country music. You know, you can go *good* in the entertainment business, too.

But country music is a way of life. If something important happens in life today, we'll probably sing it tomorrow. The music is as important to us as our instruments. At times, we protect those instruments with everything that's in us. And, at other times, we give them away. It's a strange business. I carried a Steiner fiddle all over the world, but I gave it to Os because he had been with me for so long. I wanted him to have it. Today I play a Mittenwall that Charlie Collins and Os found in a junk pile. Charlie put some iodine on it to brighten it up, and I wouldn't take anything for it.

It's all in how you look at things, I guess. Just like the

Minnie Pearl and I on stage. (WSM photo by Les Leverett)

instrument itself. If I pick it up, it's a fiddle; if Rubinoff picks up the same instrument, it's a violin.

Some of these new boys should have to go with Bill Monroe or somebody like that for a while. They'd learn what show business is. He's in his seventies and still going strong. And Ernest Tubb, he'd wear some of these young boys down in no time at all. He's still traveling all the time. Why, he's got a regular paper route. He's been going to the same places night after night, year after year.

Somebody asked Ernest recently why he still works so hard and why he still does so many one-night stands. I liked his answer: "What else would I do?" Then he added, "Why quit? I'd just be back again. Why, I've seen Roy Acuff retire five times in the last fifteen years."

He's right. What else would we do? I'm not traveling too much anymore; oh, a few dates here and there, but mostly I'm right here at the Opry all the time. I've even got a museum of stringed instruments at Opryland—one of the biggest collections of its kind in the world. It's down to where we don't have to risk our lives on the road anymore. Os and Charlie are occupied in the Opryland park; Howdy Forrester is playing on weekends with us and working at Acuff-Rose during the week.

We've been friends for a long time, and we're all still together. Most of us, anyway. We're all very happy. I guess we've come to the end of the road.